D1795600

BUCKINGHAMSHIRE
COUNTY COUNCIL

This book has been
withdrawn from the
County Library stock
Price:

35
C

3-6

L.28

TELEWORKING

TELEWORKING

A STRATEGIC GUIDE FOR MANAGEMENT

STEVEN BURCH

BUCKS COUNTY LIBRARY

MEN 5290926

S

658.4 BUR

KOGAN PAGE

First published in 1991

Apart from any fair dealing for the purposes of research or private study, or criticism or review, as permitted under the Copyright, Designs and Patents Act, 1988, this publication may only be reproduced, stored or transmitted, in any form or by any means, with the prior permission in writing of the publishers, or in the case of reprographic reproduction in accordance with the terms of licences issued by the Copyright Licensing Agency. Enquiries concerning reproduction outside those terms should be sent to the publishers at the undermentioned address:

Kogan Page Limited
120 Pentonville Road
London N1 9JN

© Steven Burch, 1991

British Library Cataloguing in Publication Data
A CIP record for this book is available from the British Library.

ISBN 0 7494 0137 0

Printed in England by Clays Ltd., St Ives plc

Contents

Preface

I wrote this book in the hope of influencing decision makers. My starting point is the conviction that teleorganising can be a viable route to lead managers out of structural problems within the organisation, and in some cases towards new business opportunities.

What makes this possible is the phenomenal transformation in the world of telecommunications and computing, which carries with it the risk of leaving those of us who are not technocrats on the sidelines, capable only of reacting to initiatives taken by others.

But technology is only a part of telework, and often more fundamental to the success of a project is the new dynamic that has to occur within a teleworking group. It is people, harnessing technology, that make it work.

The book is in three parts. The early chapters trace the origins and evolution of conventional work practices, and highlight the pressures which point to its demise as the sole model for work organisation. The middle chapters explore existing teleschemes – some old, some new – across a range of organisation types. The final chapters provide practical guidance on how to evaluate a teleproposal, how to get a scheme off the ground, and how to manage telework in the long haul when the honeymoon period is over.

I suggest that you read them in that order, remembering that the sections are short enough to read, perhaps on consecutive days, particularly if your working and home lives are punctuated by lengthy and perhaps tedious commuting by rail. However, if you are concerned more with the 'how' than the 'why', perhaps you may wish to skip the first section.

You may want to go further once you have read this book. If so, for a good grounding read Francis Kinsman's book *The Telecommuters*, or the more recent work by Huws and co-authors, *Telework: Towards the Elusive Office*. These are both important books reviewing case histories and European facts and figures on telework respectively, and I have referred to them both in this book.

Another route may be to talk to consultants. I wanted to make this book as complete and yet concise a guide to telework as possible, with the right balance between detail and reference to further help. There are several reputable consultancies, including my own, which may be of help.

TELEWORKING

By the end of the book I hope to have convinced you that teleorganising could be a niche strategy for you as you shape your organisation for its future, and that you will have the conviction to go ahead.

Acknowledgements

Writing a book on teleorganisation has been a living experiment in the practice of the art. I need to thank my brother Tony, who first introduced me to the subject. Having needed to spend many hours as a lone teleworker in the preparation of this manuscript has taught me the need for human contact, in the form of a chat and a cup of coffee. For that I thank Trish Owen, my secretary at our teleoutpost in Totnes, who always provided both when I dropped in unexpectedly.

Similarly I want to thank Barbara Dunton, my personal assistant, who works from her home near Winchester. Her help in getting the manuscript ready for publication, and indeed for writing the epilogue, is much appreciated and invaluable.

I have talked to many people on the subject, and select a few for special mention. Gary Donnison of British Telecom Western Region tried hard to explain modern telecommunications to me, and the staff of the Oftel library in Holborn provided every assistance in my search for information.

Sue Halbert, Gordon Edwards, Mike Kirby, Peter James, Stuart Dennison, Colin Fearon, Horace Mitchell, Andrew Page and Ashley Dobbs, all busy people, gave me their time in talking about their respective teleworking schemes. In preparing the book, their experience, advice and guidance have been a great strength for which I am profoundly grateful.

Finally I would like to thank my wife, Nicola, whose support and encouragement – and occasional badgering – helped to ensure that the manuscript was in the hands of the publishers on time.

Bulleigh Barton, Devon
May 1991

Acknowledgements

Part I
Why Telework?

INTRODUCTION: THE EVOLUTION OF CONVENTIONAL WORK PRACTICES

The changes in the nature of work, and the mismatch of skills available for the 1990s, have caused many organisations to consider how best to secure their futures in what increasingly looks like a very different sort of workplace.

Technology in the form of modern telecommunications and the increasingly ubiquitous use of data processing, is ravaging the boundaries of work and the way in which it is delivered.

1

Rearguard Action

We live in a moment of history where change is so speeded up that we see the present only when it is already disappearing.

RD Laing

1989 – FOUR VIGNETTES

Peter Tipton runs his own company – Monteagle, now a £2.5m business – from his home in Hampshire. He relies heavily on telecommunications technology, his fax machine and telex in order to conduct an international chemicals business. His wife is a vital personality in the business. The 24-hour world, the need to spend perhaps 100 days per year overseas, and the fact that most of the business is done over the phone really makes an 'office', as we might describe it, unnecessary.

Helen Pharoah works for ICL, the computer company, but not in the conventional sense. She is a technical author writing computer manuals for ICL's computer hardware customers. Happily, the arrangements made by ICL's home-working subsidiary, CPS, mean that remote working can be a practical route for women wanting to match the calls of raising a family with their desire to pursue a career. 'I wanted to be here for the children, around on holidays and sports days.' All this is possible from her home in Dorset. She is an employee, with normal company benefits provided on a pro rata basis to the hours she works.

Jeffrey Martin graduated in computer science, but then shunned the lure of a high salary because that would have meant working in London. He decided to remain at home in Antrim: 'Number one, it is home; number two, you might earn more in London but you have to find somewhere to live.' The attraction is the opportunity to develop a career in computing, working for international clients, which is the growing reality as his employer, BIS Beecom, develops. The company is owned by Paul McWilliams, who sees Ireland as an electronic office well placed in international time zones to service the American continent and the new-shape post-1992 Europe.

Sue Coryndon is a Management Adviser working from her home in Somerset. Her office, or rather that of The Industrial Society, is in

Eastleigh, Hampshire. She has associate status, which means that her advisory work is part of a wider portfolio, including that for other employers. All her administrative support and back-up is provided from Eastleigh. She considers that it isn't really a problem if you get the organisation right and begin to think of remote workers as the norm, which means that you manage from a different perspective. She spends one or maybe two days a week each month in the office, and notes: 'They're structured days, very interactive, and force you to make good use of your time. It works for me'.

WHO ARE THE TELEWORKERS?

There is a lot of talk about teleworking (some would say more talk than telework). But the reality is that as we proceed into this new decade it has become a normal way of work for hundreds of thousands of people in the UK.

Getting agreement about exactly what teleworking is – its extent and indeed its relevance in today's working environment – promoted a welter of debate in the academic circles of the 1970s and 1980s. This has now evolved into the community of managers and decision makers, shaping their organisations to face what increasingly looks like a very different future. But what exactly is it?

Is it home-working by telephone, a thinly veiled attempt to drive women back into the home after many years of struggle to escape domestic servitude? Is it about the right to work, or some vision of Utopia where opportunities really *are* equal?

Is it a peripheral, socially-motivated action on the part of organisations ready to stretch out a hand to a rich pool of labour which finds it difficult to attend work in offices and factories, either because of disability or the need to be home-based in order to raise a family?

Could it be a hi-tech whirlwind, here today and gone tomorrow, leaving in its wake a scrapheap of hand held telephones, lap top computers, satellite dishes, and statements from the telebank? Whatever did happen to the C5, you might say – that odd little mode of transport that was going to revolutionise personal transportation? Wrong market? Wrong time? Who knows?

Or could it be an evolving phenomenon with the potential to transform the world of work for most of us? Could the telephone line in its new digital form, fibre optic technology, and peripheral equipment create a new social and workplace revolution, which will make the organisations of the future very different from those of today?

Teleworking means different things to different people. The vignettes opening this chapter indicate that, and encapsulate the activities of entrepreneurs – those wishing to bolster a full home life with work, those exploiting the opportunities in communications technology to restructure how work is organised, and those for whom it is just a normal way of life.

A precise definition will always be too clumsy for new forms of work which are of themselves imprecise, but try this one.

> . . . Focusing work towards the individual, creatively, beyond the bounds of conventional organisational thinking, by exploiting the converging telecoms and computer technology.

For a growing number of people, both in the UK and globally, it is already happening. In 1981 there were 660,000 home-based workers in England and Wales; according to the Henley Centre for Forecasting, this figure is expected to grow to over four million by 1995. Indeed in 1985 about 7 per cent of the UK workforce was classed as home-based. The figure for the United States is about the same.

Not all of these qualify as teleworkers by the earlier definition, but they at least work in a fashion which demonstrates that flexibility in the provision of work can benefit organisations and individuals.

WHAT THE FUTURISTS SAW

The statistical nightmare and debate in one real sense is irrelevant. For the futurists, the strategists and the planners, the crystal ball reveals some fascinating insights. They envisage:

- community work centres at which teleworkers can come in from the cold, the isolation of their home-based work stations, and engage in the social exchanges so necessary for most of us. Let us not forget that, for many, work remains as the single most important source of good friendships for people of all social classes. Technology will not replace that.

- skill registers in rural market towns, which would allow the local business exchange to market its services to clients in the cities.

Interestingly, many executives who had bought country retreats in these areas may find that they can now legitimately extend their weekend stay, perhaps working from home for their employers or, indeed, for other organisations. Wiring up a town or village in this way provides a new sense of community– a telecommunity – which allows its inhabitants to enjoy the pleasures of rural life and yet remain within reach of work.

Andrew Page, Managing Director of Protocol Communications in Totnes is working towards this vision, with a little help from Prince Charles and Business in the Community. His UK Teleworking Initiative is piloting three such business exchanges in Totnes, Dorchester and West Somerset.

Even for the less visionary, telephone technology has to be a threat to complacency. Forget the restructuring, and the creative approach to matching organisational and individual needs – telework makes sense today. Take almost any office. Look dispassionately at the range of tasks carried out there, and with certainty there will be tasks which, organised differently, could be dealt with effectively from home.

MANAGEMENT WATERSHEDS

This sort of analysis is not for the faint-hearted because once a few bits of the jigsaw have been rearranged, some successes have been notched up and more people begin to like the idea of the changes. But take care. From that perspective, the conventional office set-up begins to look like an increasingly unattractive means of doing business; for some, an expensive anachronism.

Why should this be so? Mainly because many of the reasons for the huddling together of work activities no longer hold water. Some of the economic reasons included the benefits from scale economies, the need to communicate rapidly, and the shared use of capital-intensive equipment.

Undoubtedly these have been powerful arguments, especially for manufacturing where the notion that big is somehow best, and therefore beautiful, has underpinned cultural thinking in many countries. It may be that until now, best has meant big simply because labour had to be amalgamated around machinery.

What also happened, because technology offered no alternative, is that all the functions needed to support manufacturing, processing or whatever, also became amalgamated on the same site. So the office workers, the accountants, the administrators, the staff managers and the clerical workers also went to work to a locus of activity, usually right next door to the production plant, and often into an environment not best placed for the type of work being handled.

AN HISTORICAL BUSINESS TRIP

The notions of function, order and consistency follow on from Max Weber's organisational form of bureaucracy, in which everyone had a defined task, range of duties and neatly parcelled area of decision making. This structure is designed to ensure efficiency as a result of a high level of centralised control. It worked, but today it works less well because a central pillar for the support of the system is stability – a commodity in short supply in these times of endemic cultural and workplace change.

By the mid 1950s, managers turned their attention from structure to productivity. Underpinning this drive were the writings and thoughts of the school of scientific managers, such as Frederick Taylor, Henri Fayol and Max Weber. The belief was that efficiency and productivity resulted purely from sound administrative and production systems.

The 'Hawthorne Experiment' and other initiatives by free thinkers led to the rise of the human relations school. For many this meant a rethink in how to create improved morale and better work conditions, but probably only as a bolster to the drive for productivity.

By the late 1980s, the power of the individual in determining to a large degree the nature of the work contract had become established and was set to continue. Vanguard organisations learned to capitalise on this trend and to provide the best rewards for the stakeholders in the enterprise.

YESTERDAY'S MANAGERS

Back in the management era when structure was the driving force, it is easy to cast a critical eye at what we might see as inappropriate systems. But perhaps we do Weber a disservice when we criticise his organisational form.

Interestingly, the word 'office', one of the cornerstones of the system, was applied to people rather than buildings, those with 'a position or appointment involving special duties, a position of authority or trust'. No mention of office space, the nine-to-five routine, or the tea trolley.

Although bureaucracy as a practice, rather than as model, has largely fallen from grace, many of its trappings have not. One of the most punishing is touched on here.

As management skills and techniques have evolved over the last 100 years, many organisations are only now focusing their vision on results achieved rather than time consumed in work activities. In other words, measuring output rather than input.

Sadly, too much management practice is bubbling in the evolutionary soup of the earlier eras of management; pervading a depressingly large number of organisations, and the minds of managers and supervisors, is their obsession with measuring inputs to work. Control is the only strategy. Close supervision is the only tactic.

From this perspective the magnitude of change lying ahead looks like a nightmare. Work, like shifting sands, is ever changing. It could be that too many managers have their heads stuck firmly in it.

So where does our notion of teleworking leave us? Perhaps the issue is not technology but rather the fact that as we race towards the turn of the century, management is on the threshold of a transformation.

For the clear of vision and bold of heart, teleorganising could be the route to organisational excellence and individual fulfilment. For the more timid this could, as they say, just open up a whole new can of worms.

THE WORKPLACE IN FLUX

Within the last 25 years a major area of human activity has emerged – that of information processing. Its rate of expansion is such that its doubling time may be less than six years.

This reality has caused a major shift in employment patterns throughout the developed world, away from industry, the processing of energy and materials, into the processing of information. Figure 1.1 details the change for the USA, but the trends are probably true for any developed nation.

Increasingly, work will be delivered into the hands and minds of those with the right technical and interpersonal skills. Aspects of work and segments of people's responsibilities will become detached from the need to be confined in an office. How this new work is to be organised is the real challenge for management.

What will also happen, and is indeed already happening, is that as the international global digital highway is developed, it becomes increasingly easy to siphon off this information-based work from its geographical origin. Half a dozen or so American firms are now using Ireland as an electronic 'back office' for much of their data input work; at least three London Metropolitan Boroughs have remote offices in the north and south-west of England, easing their recruitment and staff retention problems.

If many of the changes so far illustrated have a longer-term aspect, most managers in Britain cannot fail to have had drawn to their attention the implications of the falling school rolls for the early years of the 1990s, which leads us to the next major driving force.

ARE YOU READY FOR THE NUMBERS GAME?

This was the title of a pamphlet produced by the Training Commission in 1989. It cajoles employers into facing the consequences of the falling birthrate since the baby boom of the 1960s. Their advice is the understand

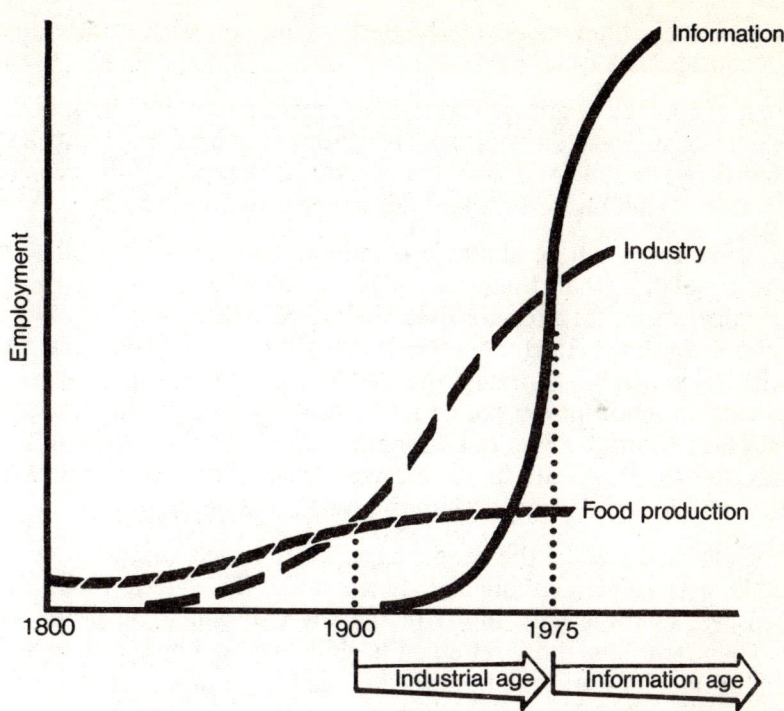

Source: Russell P (1988) *The Awakening Earth – The Global Brain.*

Employment statistics for the USA show that in 1800, prior to the Industrial Revolution, 80 per cent of the work-force was employed in food production. By 1900 the two had equalled, with about 38 per cent being employed in both sectors. This shift has continued and today food production takes up only 3 per cent of the employment.

Recently a new and more rapid growth has appeared – information processing. It has a doubling time of around six years and in 1975 overtook industry in terms of employment. Information is now the dominant form of employment in the developed nations.

Figure 1.1 Changes in the number of people involved in food production – industrial and information processing

the demographic time bomb, and to start coping now with handling it. Let us consider the facts.

- First of all, look at growth. The OECD reported recently that growth was at its strongest for a decade. For Britain the local picture means that between 1988 and 2000 the workforce is expected to grow by about one million, or by about 3.5 per cent to 28.5 million.

- By 1995 there will be almost one million fewer 16–19 year olds in the population than there are today – a fall of 25 per cent. Youth unemployment has already halved since 1982. There were 3.7 million school leavers in 1981. By 1995 there will be only 2.6 million. So with fewer people entering the system, and the prospect of real growth in job numbers, we could be heading for a yawning labour numbers shortage of up to two million people by the middle of the next decade. Where are these new recruits going to come from? Well, that rather depends, but there are several possibilities.

- Look around you. Of the people expected to be working in the year 2000, over 70 per cent are already employed. If we are to retain the prospect of these jobs, much of the shortfall will be made up by women returners, those retrained in skills required by the changing complexion of work, and from the disabled community. Alternatively the work, rather than being contained in the UK, could as we have seen be siphoned off into the global telecommunications network. This new work, largely information based, could vanish more rapidly than our manufacturing base.

Of course the UK does not have an overall shortage of manpower. What exists is a gulf between the labour market's requirements and the pool of people ready, willing and able to present themselves for work.

Take first of all the pool of unemployed. The reality is that many of these have been marooned by industries that have become outdated and have therefore failed. Others will have had to rationalise. Investment in buildings, capital equipment, and markets have not of themselves saved the day. A rearguard action to invest in people has come too late, if at all.

Therefore the first strategy will probably read something like 'Train the people to fit the jobs', which has been the battle cry of the Training Commission. This is big, long-term investment, which is focused on re-skilling individuals to fit into new jobs in organisations, some of which have limited perspectives about how work should be delivered.

The idea that work can be delivered leads us to a second strategy. Our current myopic orientation towards work classifies people in the main as employed or unemployed. The term 'unemployable' is used to cover that large pool of workers cast adrift in our earlier scenario. Their skills do not fit the new technology.

Perhaps we should change our orientation, and use the term 'unemployable' to describe organisations rather than individuals – those organisations which have failed to invest in designing ways in which work can be delivered to those for whom 'going to work' is not a realistic prospect.

Create or Abdicate is the title of a report by the Institute of Manpower Studies. Their resonant message is: 'Create appropriate employment strategies or abdicate your place in the market'.

Some more statistics are set out below.

■ The *Labour Market Quarterly Review*, January 1989 says that virtually all the increase in the labour force to the year 2000 is projected to be accounted for by women, many of whom will be returning to the labour market after having children; by 2000 it is expected that 74 per cent of women of working age will be in the labour force (51 per cent in 1971). The report further says that the increasing desire of women to continue in paid employment has been helped by the increased number of part time jobs – apart from those formally in the labour force a significant number of women (nearly one million) would like regular paid work, but could not look for it because of family commitments. Clearly there is some scope here for some innovative means of providing work on a remote basis. But how could the disabled help?

■ The 1988 Spring Labour Force survey revealed that 1.5 million of us had work-limiting health problems. The biggest category of disability (42 per cent) reported problems with limbs or back. The second largest category (11 per cent) were those with chest, breathing or asthmatic problems. Heart, blood, and circulatory complaints accounted for 9 per cent of reasons. From our new perspective, we can see that sensitively designed programmes ought to allow organisations to unlock these hidden abilities, where perhaps there are only three major constraints on the ability of the individual to join in working: first, the ability to travel to an office; second, the ease of accommodation within the office, and third, the ability of the person to allocate eight or nine hours of the working day at a fixed time.

■ Finally, before we move on to lament the increasing difficulty people are finding in simply getting to work, consider for a moment just what the 'shifting sands' of work actually means. The Institute for Employment Research forecasts that overall growth in employment between 1988 and 2000 will be about 8.6 per cent. This is about double the levels predicted in the *Employment Gazette*. More interesting are the changes in the type of employment, the table below showing the percentage change of employment in various sectors.

Employment change 1988–2000 (%)			
Losers		*Winners*	
Agriculture	−11	Construction	+14
Mining	−23	Distribution	+ 5
Utilities	−21	Hotels and catering	+20
Metals, minerals	− 9	Transport and communication	+12
Engineering	−10	Business services	+15
Food, drink and tobacco	−20	Miscellaneous services	+55
Textiles and clothing	−23	Health and education	+10
		Public administration	+ 3

As well as the significant swing in industry types, (a skill shift away from manual and towards cerebral activity), the changes in occupational types also mirror this trend.

The final observation and statistical comment results from a study by McKinsey's in 1986 which estimated that by the year 2020, 70 per cent of all jobs in Europe would require cerebral rather than manual skill. Not only is that a reversal of the figures from only 50 years ago but also it begins to point to new panoramas for job organisation, networking and telework. See Figure 1.2.

Figure 1.2 illustrates this trend for the USA with over 50 per cent of the total workforce employed in information processing.

CONGESTION

This was the stark title of an alarming report from The Institute of Civil Engineers, which pointed to a dire future for those relying in particular on the road system as their means of travelling to work.

The conurbations are becoming victims of their own economic success. The concentration of work into towns and cities is a strong magnet, with tremendous pull for those wishing to reap the rewards for a considerable sacrifice in travelling time. For many workers, matching the desire to work in the city is the desire to live outside it. Modern transportation makes that possible.

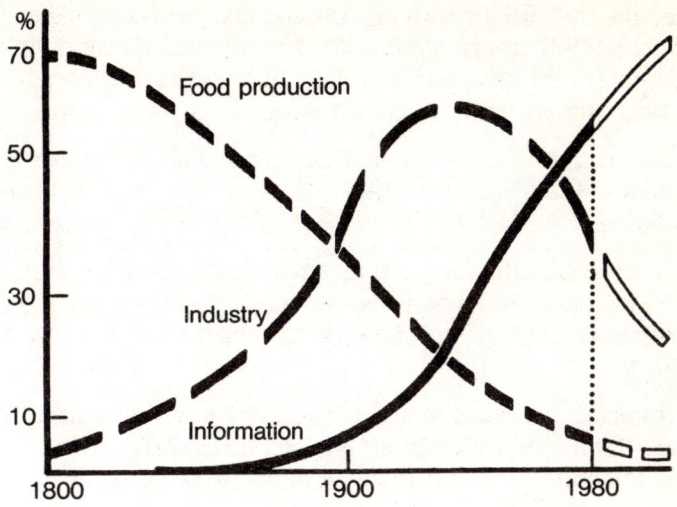

The same data as Figure 1.1, the number of people employed in agriculture, industry and information processing being plotted as the percentage of the total workforce. This brings out more clearly the relative changes in each area. In the late 1800s, about 50 per cent were in agriculture; in the 1930s over 50 per cent in industry; in the 1980s over 50 per cent in information processing (data applies to USA).

Figure 1.2 The workplace in flux

But will it be so in the future? The experiences of commuters in London are at the hub of the problem. For some, it is quicker to commute by InterCity from Bristol to central London than it is to travel from Kent or even from the East End.

The average commuter spends 190 minutes per week commuting to and from work. London commuters spend 295 minutes – the rough equivalent of spending six working weeks each year, just getting to work. Better rail and road links amplify the problem as they inexorably suck in even more travellers to the hub of congestion.

The growth in Gross Domestic Product (GDP) and the growth of expenditure on passenger traffic are closely linked – indeed both have grown by 27 per cent between 1977 and 1987. Consider some other facts.

- Since the early 1950s travel by car and taxi has increased by 900 per cent. By 1987 there were over 19 million cars and light vans licensed. In the five years to 1987, rail travel as a whole grew by 26 per cent and air travel by 38 per cent.

- London commuting in the morning peak time has increased by 10 per cent in the five years to 1987 – the use of private cars to commute has fallen.

- BR Network South-East has recorded increases of 19 per cent since 1982 in peak time arrivals. London Underground traffic has increased beyond all expectations: passenger kilometres up by 70 per cent.

- BR InterCity volumes varied between narrow limits until 1985, at about 12 billion passenger kilometres. In 1987–88 this statistic had risen to about 13.3 – an increase of about 11 per cent.

- A salutory fact which helps to explain why at least one courier firm in the city now has 'runners' rather than 'riders' is that traffic on London's roads has increased by about 1 per cent per annum since 1976. Vehicle speeds have steadily declined and are now down to about 11.5 mph.

London is clogging up. But the rest of the major conurbations seem to have similar, if smaller-scale, problems. Average city driving speeds in Newcastle, Glasgow, Sheffield, Birmingham and Leeds are not much higher than in central London. Congestion is now returning to Manchester and Glasgow after the imaginative motorway and by-pass schemes of the 1970s provided temporary relief.

Congestion, the report by the Institute of Civil Engineers (1989) attempts to cost this level of congestion; those pertinent to business include the following beliefs.

- Congestion encourages businesses to hold a higher level of inventory. This could amount to about £200m per week – (protagonists of 'Just in Time' inventory control take note.)

- Congestion means more but less serious smashes – the cost of vehicle accidents to businesses exceeds £2 billion per year.

- The biggest resource waste is time. According to a British Road Federation Survey, the total congestion costs in Greater London for 1987–88 amounted to an estimated £3168m. Of this total, 72 per cent was caused by the loss of non-working time due solely to congestion.

The conclusions which flow from these findings are startling.

> An expanding economy is wearing down an inadequate infrastruc-
> ture . . . congestion will probably increase to choke point . . . con-
> gestion is itself now acting as a regulator of traffic . . . in view of the
> length of time (15 years) in the planning and construction of a new
> infrastructure . . . there is no possibility of solving congestion.

The recommendations point towards ways in which the density of traffic
can be spread, and include flexitime, four-day working, staggering school
starting times, and staggering school holidays and Bank Holidays. It also
points to home-based working as one viable strategy.

ORGANISATIONAL ECOSYSTEMS

Tunnel vision is a costly by-product of conventional thinking about
organisations. The so-called 'demographic time bomb' can be managed
in creative ways; there is no absolute shortage of skills and abilities,
except in the context of conventional 'monolithic' organisational ideas,
and ways of employing people.

The prerequisite that people must travel to work to somehow be
employable is a devastatingly short-sighted approach by organisations
facing a skills shortage. The same lack of logic leads to the pervading
convention of working from about 8 or 9 am to about 5 or 6 pm.

From this perspective, it should therefore come as absolutely no surprise that a report by ACAS, the Advisory, Conciliation and Arbitration
Service, should find that 'flexible working hours can improve profits, job
satisfaction and motivation and can attract talented employees
unwilling to work a normal 9–5 day.'

Flexibility, complexity, and designing the organisation of work from
the individual perspective seems to be part of the answer to capturing
the productivity of people. Birmingham City Council understands this
well and began a job-sharing scheme in 1983 as a job creation policy in a
time of high unemployment. This policy, according to Stephen Ward,
their Executive Director for Personnel, is now an important recruitment
and retention measure and is encouraging that organisation to experiment
with flexibility, at a senior level; in November 1989 they began advertising
for a city treasurer, at a salary of £62,000, with job sharing as an option.

These and other 'win, win' employment deals mean that the future for
organisations begins to look safest in the hands of those who have developed 'organisational ecosystems', which shun simple solutions and
accept that flexibility in the provision of work is one way of reducing the

'hot spots' that can otherwise develop. We can see how the intensive business world of the big conurbations has caused these 'hot spots' for travel, for costs of accommodation, and in general for the quality of life. Flexible work organisation, including tele-initiatives, will ease the pressure, and introduce controlling mechanisms such as those that regulate the natural world.

BACK TO THE OFFICE

Continuing this evolutionary business trip, as the 1990s unfold, it may well be that the search for greater productivity again causes us to focus on the office. Conservative estimates, according to Bruce Lloyd, writing in *Management Today*, suggest that of the workforce in the UK, between 25 and 50 per cent currently work in offices. That implies a tremendous resource, perhaps one-third of the nation's GDP, tied up in this activity in one form or another.

To date competitive pressures have not really required much investigation into the use of this most precious of assets. Many offices are noisily unproductive by day, and expensively empty by night. Few are probably effectively occupied for more than about 20 per cent of the year; in terms of real work carried out, a figure of 5 to 10 per cent is probably nearer the mark. 'No-one', continues Bruce Lloyd, 'running a factory, coal mine or power station would be allowed to operate at these levels of use'.

One way to avoid the high costs of corporate life in these 'hot spots' is to move out, and the partial exodus from London has already begun, with the biggest occupier of office space in London – the government – relocating part of its activities to the regions. Shell UK has plans to move 500 staff out of the Strand, following BP and Esso. Mercury Communications is planning part of its expansion programme into office accommodation in Milton Keynes.

Another way is take a fundamental look at what actually goes on in offices, with an injection of creativity which goes far beyond cramming more people into less space.

The results of such a rigorous analysis could be a powerfully more productive organisation, with work carried out only where it needs to be, in a flexible combination of locations and working arrangements. Those that fail and opt exclusively for the office complex solution, as Bruce Lloyd eloquently puts it, could find:

> some of the more ambitious corporate ego trips . . . at the front of
> the queue of the industrial and social dinosaurs of tomorrow.

2
Evolution of the Teledebate

However simple it becomes to communicate remotely, we cannot imagine a future in which the majority of people are not in regular social contact with each other in the course of carrying out their daily work.

Huws, Korte, and Robinson

THE EARLY DAYS

Ursula Huws and co-authors have brought the teledebate full circle in their rigorous analysis of the state of the art in telework. From early beginnings the interest, at least in the literature, was fuelled by oil price increases which opened up an arithmetical route to marvellous projections for savings to employer and employed by staying at home to work. Travelling to work was becoming expensive, in terms of both cost and time.

Jack Nilles, of the Centre for Futures Research in California, carried out studies in Los Angeles after the 1973 oil crisis into the economics of teleworking. He concluded that if just one in seven urban commuters dropped out, the US would have no need to import oil.

Latching on to these opportunities and predictions the futurists predicted the demise of conventional work organisation and a proliferation of 'electronic cottages' which would herald the start of a new kind of workplace revolution.

Cost structures change when employees cease to be exclusively office-based; the spiralling cost of office occupancy became another prime motivator in the early 1980s which encouraged organisations to look at shedding overheads.

Read *Networking in Organisations* which documents the Rank Xerox range of teleworking experiments during the early 1980s. A close examination of the direct and indirect costs of occupancy of London-based accommodation staggered the authors, and became a prime motivator for the search for new solutions in the provision of work. They challenged the belief that salaries were the major part of departmental budgets and were hence a prime area for cost cutting. For Rank Xerox at least, this was not true. Salaries accounted for only 30 per cent of their total office costs. The rest were grouped under 'facilities' 31 per cent, 'on costs and benefits' 15 per cent, and 'others' which included data processing, travel etc, 24 per cent.

In other words, at face value it began to appear that basing an employee in an office, saddled the organisation with a bill of about 2½ times the salary of each employee. Figure 2.1 opposite is developed from the Rank Xerox original.

Some of the costs, of course, would accompany every employee working on a telebasis (for example travel, data processing, heat and light etc) but much of the burden associated with the building could be reduced. It would be a mistake, however, to assume that knowledge of occupancy costs is common currency; as part of the research carried out for this book, 278 of the largest London-based employers were asked for their views on how much they would be prepared to pay for fully serviced offices, in comparison with their existing occupancy costs. Of the few who responded, most had little idea of their true costs, or at least were coy about disclosing the information.

A rerun of the Rank Xerox calculation may well serve as an incentive to explore telework, or as a benchmark against which to evaluate options. Clearly, all other things being equal (but remember that they never are) there is a very steep cost gradient away from London, which can be exploited by the various forms of telework.

OUT OF THE FRYING PAN . . .

Anecdotes abounded in the literature of the 1970s and 1980s, based on the experience of those involved in this way of working. Two Titans of the literature, Alvin Toffler and Tom Forrester, embraced the main elements of the debate. In fact Toffler dreamed up the notion of the 'electronic cottage'.

> We are about to revolutionise our homes . . . a return to cottage industry on a new, higher, electronic basis, and with it a new emphasis on the home as the centre of society . . . powerful forces are converging to promote the electronic cottage.

Heady stuff, and typical of the side of the debate which sees new technology as the key in delivering work back to homes as a part of the continuing evolution of work. The office may have been, the protagonists might argue, nothing more than a temporary aberration.

Rank Xerox – 1982

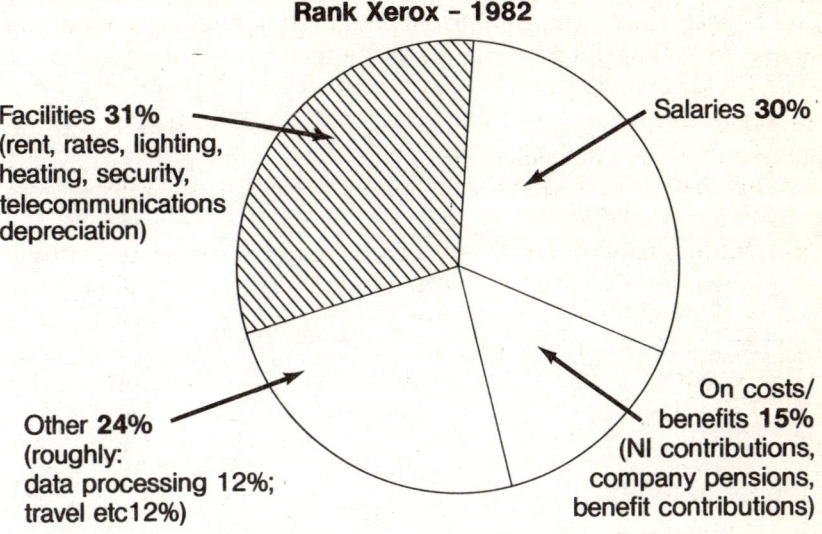

Facilities **31%**
(rent, rates, lighting,
heating, security,
telecommunications
depreciation)

Salaries **30%**

Other **24%**
(roughly:
data processing 12%;
travel etc12%)

On costs/
benefits **15%**
(NI contributions,
company pensions,
benefit contributions)

Source: Rank Xerox Limited, 1982

Your Organisation – 1991?

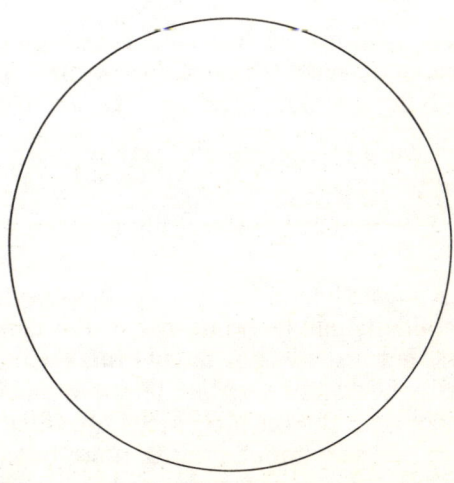

Figure 2.1. Cost structures in organisations

This line of thought, particularly the aspect of growth, has not gone unchallenged. Some of the wilder projections for home telework may never be met. Most commentators feel the need to offer explanations for the relatively slow uptake of the idea. Tom Forrester, writing in *Futures* in 1988, and based partly on his own experience as a teleworker, explains one reason for this.

> Most important of all in my view, the literature (with a few honourable exceptions) glosses over and seriously underestimates the psychological problems of working at home.

He goes on to suggest that many people, after a honeymoon period of perhaps two years, drift back to a conventional mode of work.

Throughout the 1980s the number of teleworkers has grown, and with it a rash of survey work which has attempted to underpin the emotional argument with hard facts. Some of these are unpalatable – especially for the media, which often maintains a romance with the idea out of all proportion with reality.

. . . AND INTO THE FIRE

- Telework at home can lead to isolation, when jobs and job holders are evicted from the office. Sitting at home in isolation without proper preparation can be very demotivating and stressful.

- To outsiders, telework might sound as though you can get nothing else. Your friends might show sympathy for something they cannot understand: 'Never mind, dear, a proper job will turn up soon'.

- If you are a male teleworker, you may possibly expect to have your own home office, and a wife who protects you from children and other distractions such as washing up, neighbours, and odd jobs around the house.

- If you are a female teleworker you will be expected to run the home, tend the children, and telework – all at the same time. You know it won't work, but just try convincing others who have seen you cope marvellously. Combining serious telework and child-raising is not likely to work well. The benefits of telework come from the productive work environment without interruptions from children. Telework may mean using the services of a nursery or a child minder.

- Many disabled people are more likely than other groups to seek work for social reasons. Home-working without careful design is not helpful here, as it traps many disabled people in the environment from which they need a break.

- Opting for telework outside the main office environment could be just about terminal for your career prospects – this is a fear of many who feel that they are leaving the main stream of activity and are likely to be by-passed.

Attitudes harden when benefits are questionable, and take time to change. Taking work outside the conventional organisation, out of the reach of much of the cosseting legislative framework and beyond the control of unions, made home-working look like exploitation which, for many, is exactly what it turned out to be. Even now it is impossible to conduct a debate with some union representatives without reference to sweat-shops and general exploitation.

Quite often the home-workers were women without options. Raising families created the need for greater income on the one hand and took away on the other hand their ability to go out and earn it. So, a niche employment market was created with an array of conditions, almost inevitably less favourable to home-workers than to those within the conventional framework.

The legacy that home-working is bad news is a persistent thought in many minds, particularly those responsible for a watching brief over collective rights and those responsible for managing. Strangely enough, the possibility of spending at least part of the working week at home is a tantalising prospect for many. Field the argument that it allows women to manage career breaks more effectively, or that it reduces the commut -ing toll, or any other window-dressing attractions, and teleworking seems to make sense.

Almost in spite of the polemics, teleworking has been evolving since the 1960s. Mrs Steve Shirley, the doyenne of teleworkers, set up F International in 1962 as a means of allowing her to manage the dual calls of family and career. She now controls the 20th largest software house in Britain with an annual growth rate of over 30 per cent. Over 1300 staff at present work for what is now know as the FI group, largely on a self-employed basis – mainly women, and mainly working from home. More of the FI group later.

DIFFERENT MOTIVATIONS

What leads organisations to consider teleworking schemes? There are a variety of motivators which are common neither among organisations nor fixed in time. Sometimes schemes are developed after a great deal of

planning and careful preparation. Others seem to evolve almost by seren-
dipity, when the aspirations of individuals happily coalesce with those of
employers. Gil Gordon, an American telework consultant, rates eight
motivators for organisations taking this route:

- improved recruitment

- curiosity to experiment

- hiring the disabled

- employee demand

- improved retention of staff

- space savings

- increased productivity

- improved customer service.

The European perspective is provided by Ursula Huws, in the survey of
14 organisations operating teleworking schemes of one kind or another.
They asked managers responsible for those schemes to rank a list of
fifteen possible motivators. Clear 'front runners' were:

- an improved ability to cope with work peaks

- retention and recruitment of scarce skills.

'Pipped at the post' were:

- reduction of turnover

- opportunity to combine work and child care

- improved staff motivation and productivity.

The 'also rans', favoured by about one-third of managers were:

- reduction in central office and overhead costs

- flexibility in working hours

- reduction in commuting.

Of course these motivators are not discrete unconnected factors. There is
a mishmash of cause and effect. One construction is that the front runners,
work peaks and staff shortages, are merely symptoms of an illness
caused by the sort of conventional 'organisation think' covered in Chapter 1. In reality this is simple cause and effect.

Cause . . .

- bunch people together in cities
- make them travel a long way
- constrain them to a 'normal' working day
- deny many the opportunity to combine family and career goals
- make them all employees.

. . . and effect:

- high occupancy costs
- sub-optimum productivity
- low morale
- skill shortage
- low flexibility to deal with peaks and troughs.

Not surprisingly, managers within the organisation relate to these latter factors, rather than the fundamental causes, which are the hallmarks of conventional organisation.

From the employee perspective, though, the issue has a rather different appearance. They home in on the causes of their dissatisfaction with their existing working arrangements or, for those denied access to conventional work, to the barriers which prevent them from taking it up. So their ranking of motivators is likely to include:

- the need for flexibility in combining work and non-work;
- the desire for autonomy, possibly within an employed framework, or the prospect of becoming self-employed and contracting to organisations;
- the prospect of much reduced commuting;
- lifestyle demands;
- limited alternative work options, where individuals are constrained by priorities other than the conventional work option, eg raising families, caring for relatives etc.

Clearly, their concerns are not those of the organisation, nor are they possible to rank in any sensible order. An employee itching to run her own show for example, with a strong desire for autonomy, may be without a family, or indeed a long daily journey to work. For her, the need to reduce the length of commuting time or reconcile home and family life are not simply low priority motivators. They are actually irrelevant.

Certainly, in the case of the examples covered later, the sequence of events seems to be that employers initiate and workers respond. But this has not been an exclusive one-way tide, and it is possible to envisage circumstances in which the complete reverse is true – for example where employers are chasing particularly scarce skills. This is already happening, and at present there is developing a secondary job market for teleworkers who can now change jobs without relocating.

Equally, key individuals can have an important influencing role on their managers in devising a scheme, as was the case for the Digital Equipment Company, where a valued employee wishing to continue to work for the company was able to do so after devising a scheme with her boss. This is an arrangement which has become a model for a more extensive teleworking programme.

Employer motivations are not fixed in time, and though they may be the reasons for initiating schemes, they are rarely because of philanthropy or as experiments but most likely in response to business problems or marketing opportunities. Let us look at how these motivations have changed with time. Table 2.1 opposite attempts to link the prevailing business climate with organisations taking the teleroute as a means of work provision.

PARADIGMS

Each of us develops our own perspectives and unwritten rules about how to do things, and the same is true of organisations. Paradigms are rules such as these, that we take for granted, and underpin the assumptions about how we live and work.

History is littered with the wreckage of those, such as the cable moguls of the latter part of the nineteenth century, who believed that their telegraph circuits around the world would never be replaced by the novelty of the telephone. They failed to challenge their own paradigms and continued to see the world exactly as they wished to see it.

Anyone burdened with the responsibility of managing any sort of organisational change will be familiar with the entrenched attitudes and myopic perspectives which create walls of resistance to new ideas in spite of their intrinsic value. Equally, anyone tasked with the responsibility of making sound project evaluations will be skilled in examining the weaknesses in every 'hair-brained' scheme which comes along.

For some, the teledebate will become one of these schemes, and there is a danger that the language of the debate will become purely one of

Table 2.1 A brief chronology of remote working developments

Economic or Social Factors	Organisation	Motivators
1960s and 1970s		
Start of growth in IT	F International	Marketing opportunity
Regulation of work practices by governments and unions		Work option for women
Shortage of IT skills	International Computers Ltd	Retention of skills of women leaving to have families
1980s		
Radical shake out of manufacturing slack	Cox's Pharmaceuticals	Improved customer service
Growth of information- and service-based economy	Rank Xerox	Cost-cutting experiments in new work organisation,
Economic growth leading to hot spots	Texas	Meeting individual goals
Congestion	Lloyds Bank	High staff turnover
Growth of flexible working	Digital	Desire to regionalise
Growth of sub-contracting	Windsor and Maidenhead BC	To be in the vanguard of new work practise
Rising office rents and occupancy costs	Enfield BC	Acute skills shortage Fluctuation in workloads; desire to provide work in community
	Frontline Initiative	Inner city training and marketing opportunity
1990s	UK Telework Initiative	Marketing opportunity
True cost of rail transport Slow economic growth Demographic trough Open trade frontiers Global telecommunications		Pooling and selling local IT skills into organisations Flexible provision of work, possibly based around a core of key employees

cost. It is probably difficult to detach any business debate from its cost implications, but it is significant that of the schemes reviewed in this book, other than for the pioneering Rank Xerox range of projects, none had cost savings as the prime motivator.

THE MACRO VIEW

The Henley Centre for Forecasting, in its 1988 report, estimated that around half the working population could be involved in telecommuting. They extrapolate current data to 1995 and conclude that by then more than 21 million working days, or around 20 per cent of the time available, could be spent at home.

Fundamental changes in the provision of work of this order of magnitude cannot fail to impact on the economics of everyday life. Office rents, house prices, transportation costs, the availability of skilled labour, will all be affected.

We have seen the ripple effect on increased house prices as improved transport allows longer-distance commuting away from London. Part of the same trend has been the huge rise in London office space rental costs. Both of these factors result from our inability satisfactorily to disseminate work from the focus of economic activity – the 'hot spots' of Chapter 2.

Though the future may be an uncertain place to be, predictions are helpful in formulating frameworks and scenarios, or at least indicating trends. So what are the main implications of teleorganising? We can speculate, but probably not quantify, at least in the long run. What will there be more of? And less of? Take a look at the 'predictions' opposite.

Either list can be extended. Few of the items can be sensibly measured and several could be equally at home in either list. For example, take 'social interaction' – for some this is primarily office-centred, for others home-centred. Similarly, at the macro level both lists contain benefits and disadvantages.

The fact that the world is a constantly changing place further complicates forecasting. Could the sum of all the implications of teleorganisations be even discernible against the backcloth of a fundamental shift in the economy? Probably not. A downturn may well reduce the pressures to move towards teleorganisation as office rental costs and skills shortages diminish. These conditions will undermine the cost-reduction benefits for some organisations, and encourage them to remain with the *status quo*. Conversely, such a downturn might encourage others to seek new markets or, indeed, more effective means of internal organisation.

WHAT ABOUT TECHNOLOGY?

The exponential growth in telecoms and computing technology, in themselves, are not motivators for teleorganising, but the growth in capacity and the associated tumbling costs are tremendously powerful

Predictions	
More	*Less*
variety of work location	commuting
self-employment	social interaction
choice of employer	stress
disposable time	road accidents
isolation	expensive offices
telecoms and computing hardware	union organisation
development of the individual	time lost through illness
work for the intelligent	transport jobs
need for language ability	traffic jams
self-fulfilment	pollution
home accidents	shopping centres
doubling up of office space	office ritual
clean air	time wasting
appropriate management	
attention to output	
postal traffic	
home deliveries	
time with children	
integrated house design	
productivity	

facilitators, bringing the possibility of telework into the realms of a growing community of people. The few paragraphs which follow aim to paint a technological picture for the non-technical.

Analogue versus digital

The human voice is and will remain stubbornly analogue. From Bell's invention of the telephone onwards, and until relatively recently, voice transmissions have been carried in analogue form, usually along pairs of copper cables utilising a variable electric current, to reproduce the voice transmission in the receiving handset.

Computer technology evolved along a different route. The internal communication and computing relied on the binary or digital system which meant that information was represented in streams and combinations of simple 'on' or 'off' signals. Because of their speed of operation, computers could handle information effectively in this manner.

41

Problems began to arise when businesses saw the value of being able to store and transfer data from computer to computer, between buildings and across continents. In order to make this happen, digital computer language had to be translated into the analogue form which could then be sent down the telephone wires. At the distant end the process was reversed with the analogue signal being converted back to digital, such that the computer could read it.

The hardware which facilitate these translations are the modems which have proliferated wherever computers need to talk to each other across the telephone system. An analogy of their operation is in the role of translators, helping those using different languages to communicate.

It can work well, but data transmission speeds may not be quick enough for on-line use with fast computers. Similarly, using this hybrid system there is the risk of corruption of information in transmission.

The revolution in telecoms is in its adoption of the digital system, forming a common transmission language for voice and data transfer. A parallel development is evident in the world of music. Gramophone technology has led to a very high quality of reproduction via the stylus needle, the 12-inch record, and analogue technology. But there is little doubt that the compact disc offers truer reproduction. In fact, it is light years ahead – at least in the sense that it is using laser light as the medium for digital transmission.

Fibre-optic technology

Digital transmission can be generated down copper wires by switching on and off the electrical current, but fibre-optic technology now allows an altogether more attractive alternative. For communications, this application simply means shining a light down a glass cored tube, and switching the light on and off in such a way as to transmit a message. It is digital transmission using light rather than electricity.

Light, a superabundant entity, and sand, another superabundant material from which glass is derived, have allowed a quantum leap in communications from the days of paired copper wires and mechanical switching in telephone circuits. As we have seen, the light is in the form of lasers; once glass could be purified to an extent that one could see through nine miles of it, long-distance fibre-optic communications became possible. Indeed, transmission distances of up to 30 miles have been achieved across the Channel, without the need for repeaters to boost the signal.

British Telecom is working hard to convert the trunk and local networks from copper wire to fibre optics, and Mercury Communications, their rivals in the business sector, have now completed their figure-of-eight circuit around the UK giving direct service access to many large cities.

The typical fibre-optic cable is approximately 1 cm in diameter and contains ten pairs of fibres, each almost individually invisible. To get some idea of the capacity of this cable, it can handle many thousands of simultaneous phone calls, limited in the main only by the capacity of the equipment at either end of the lines.

The air waves

Microwave transmissions are commonplace; indeed, many routine phonecalls may include short radio hops, especially to outlying districts. Engineers are finding ever more ingenious ways to exploit the limited radio spectrum.

Car phones, transportables and hand-held phones were evolved from nowhere in the mid-1980s and are now used by about 800,000 people, mainly in the business community. Some of the wild-card predictions for the turn of the century suggest that there may be as many as 12 million portable phones of one sort or another in use.

The next generation of portable phones, known as CT2, was launched recently and the networks are being developed by consortia including British Telecom and Mercury, called Phonepoint and Callpoint respectively. Truly pocket-sized phones are already allowing calls to be made from within about 200 metres of the telepoint terminals that are rapidly popping up at railway stations, motorway service areas and other communications focal points. The traffic is one-way: you can call them from your pocket phone, but they cannot call you.

But this next technological hurdle may well be overcome by 1993 with the first trials of the personal communications network or PCN. This system will provide small, light, hand-held phones based on advanced digital technology, which may well offer a serious alternative to the extensive cable networks which are in operation. These developments deliver computing and telecommunications power at low cost and with few restraints on location. But there is a current development which will throw open the public network in a creative way, allowing amazing flexibility in the use of a single phone line. This is British Telecom's integrated services digital network (ISDN).

ISDN

Because of the difficulties in attempting to pump data, especially at high speeds, over the public network which have already been discussed, many organisations have set up their own data transmission networks, distinct from the public switched voice network.

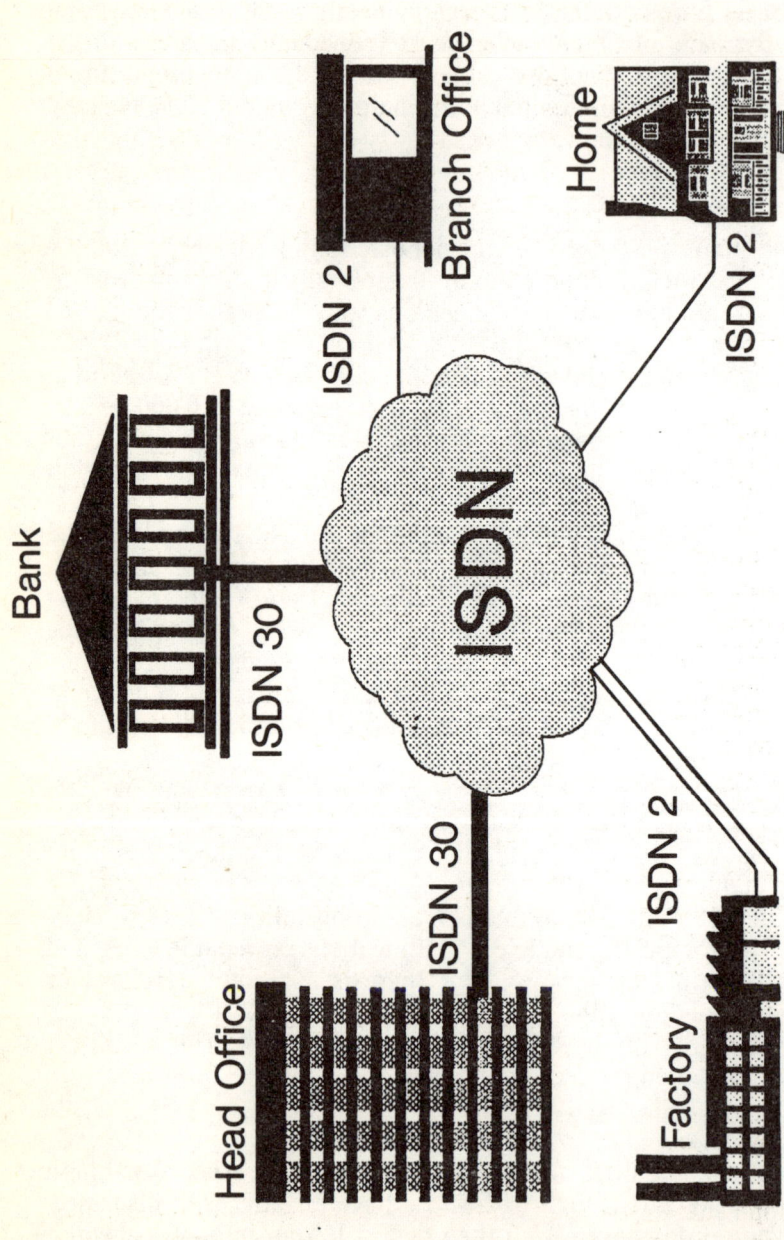

Figure 2.2. How the Integrated Services Digital Network brings telecommunications power to the home and office

Source: British Telecom

ISDN won't supersede these networks, but it will allow the whole panoply of communication requirements to be brought to your desk. Voice, data, text or image can be transported without discrimination and at very high speeds, in digital form across the public network, and without the need for modems. The system simply allows digital communication to break out from the network into the end-user's premises. Nor is size an issue: ISDN will deliver the same power to the desk of the multinational executive, the remote office worker or the home-worker.

How does it work? ISDN 2 provides two separate channels in an ordinary phoneline which allows transfer of data of 64Kbit per second – about 50 times faster than over a standard circuit. With a distribution node close to the work area, up to eight pieces of equipment can be linked although only two can be used at any one time. So it is possible to hold a telephone conversation with a remote colleague while both are viewing the same data.

The big brother of this system is ISDN 30, which is the system which will be used by large end-users, such as corporate headquarters. When linked into this the single line user commands exactly the same power and range of facilities as his or her corporate colleague.
Data can be transferred roughly seven times faster than when using the fastest modem available on the public network. A computer file that would take ten minutes to transmit at 1200 bits per second through an ordinary telephone network will take about eleven seconds using ISDN. And those ponderous fax transmissions will be speeded up with the new generation group four machines operating over the ISDN to a rate of less than four seconds per page.

ISDN is new and BT expect to provide about 90,000 lines by 1992. Regard it as a further technological breakthrough which opens up the horizons for flexible working. The 1990s look like being roller coaster years for the telecommunications industry, with an accelerating pace of developments. It is hard to imagine that the shape of many businesses will survive this onslaught.

However, telework is not fundamentally about technology beyond the ordinary telephone line. Many of the teleworking organisations have a fairly rudimentary level of internal telecoms sophistication, even though they may be working in the IT field.

The human touch

The developments in telecoms continue to deliver power into the hands and, more particularly, the minds of small organisations and networks. The result will be that many more organisations and occupations can look down the telework route – but not before the managerial, organisational and social factors have been properly mastered.

WHO DECIDES?

No doubt decision makers in organisations will, and have prided themselves on their bold decisions to teleorganise. The pioneers, notably Steve Shirley of the FI Group, are to be congratulated for their vision and perseverance but in the final analysis teleorganising is a marketing exercise, and only works in response to an identifiable need. It is all about packaging work to a segmented market.

It may or may not be cheaper than the conventional alternative, but this is only a valid comparison when the conventional alternative is available. In the examples which follow and in most tales of telework this is just not the case.

Part I: Key Point Summary

- By the year 2000 as many as 70 per cent of all jobs in Europe will require cerebral rather than manual skills, a complete reversal of the situation over the last 50 years.

- The average commuter spends the equivalent of six weeks of his or her own time each year simply in getting to work.

- Many offices are unproductive by day and expensively empty by night. Few are effectively occupied for more than about 20 per cent of the year.

- Though some of the earlier teleworking schemes were motivated by the desire to reduce the cost of central overheads, this is now less prominent in motivations for telework. The need to recruit, to retain and use staff effectively has become much more important.

- The revolution in telecoms is now creating scope for radical changes in organisation and marketing opportunities, through the development of fibre-optic technology, digital transmission, and the more extensive use of the air waves.

Part II
Track Records

INTRODUCTION: TELEWORK IN PRACTICE

When William Hudson published his new botanical classification *Flora Anglica* in 1762 he had faced and worked through the dilemma of those with a passion to divide and archive evolving life forms. It is a necessary process in the route to understanding, rather than a prescriptive mechanism, for all time.

And so it is with telework. Accepting this caveat, it is possible to filter into different streams the types of scheme that are currently operating. They have different characteristics and embrace those who are employed and self-employed. Some of the schemes are, at face value, hard to identify in that they do not resemble in any way the image of the person working at home with merely a VDU screen for company.

Teleworking is primarily about collection and distribution of information and services, which may not be place dependent. Some refer to it as 'remote working', which it most certainly is not, for the best teleworking schemes are designed to dispel the notion of remoteness, or being out of touch.

Take the word 'tele'. It means 'at a distance' or 'from far off'. This is helpful, for it embraces the notion of remoteness. But from what? The marketplace? The processing centre? The teleworker? It doesn't actually matter. Most of the problems of any type of telework classification result from thinking too parochially about the conventional organisation and its boundaries. More than anything else, teleworking allows one to shrink distances, either within the organisation such that people do not have to sit together to work together, or externally such that close contact with clients can be kept, without the need actually to be there.

In the next few chapters you will learn something of the lot of the lone teleworker, the teleoutposts, the teleco-ops and the tele-organisations.

3

The Lone Teleworkers

THE LONE TELEHUNTERS

These are the self-employed, roaming the work-plain, with a range of consulting, creative, or information-based skills on offer to organisations unable to cope with the peaks and troughs of work within their existing structure, or who have decided to 'stick to the knitting' of their main business and sub-contract out everything else.

Variously called freelancers, sub-contractors or 'one-man bands', there are several factors which put a ring fence around this group. First, they probably work for a range of clients; second, they survive and exploit a market-place dominated by conventional organisations; finally, because the individuals are usually fiercely independent, they are unlikely to form groupings or in any way challenge the existing provision of work.

Because they are so diverse in their types of work and method of operation, highlighting any individual case is probably not very instructive. However, there are lots of them out there, and many suburban streets will probably have several of them, quietly teleworking away.

THE LONE TELEWORKERS

These are a very different breed. Mainly employed, these people retain a strong umbilical link with the providing organisation, and probably work for no-one else. The existence of their jobs is usually a response by the organisation to a skills gap, and the impetus may come from a valued employee negotiating a work package with a substantial home-based element, or from the organisation taking a policy decision to offer home-working as a recruitment or retention option.

This grouping is populated by the 'matchers'. These are people in search of the right balance between their work and non-work existences. They attempt to match the calls on their time as carers in raising families or helping parents, with those of a responsible job or career. Matching also helps the disabled, where the employer attempts to provide a range of enabling conditions which allow a full contribution from the disabled person.

51

From the employers' viewpoint this is the start of a 'harvesting' technique, allowing them to reap the benefits of the skills available in the broader community at large which have been previously denied them because of their conventional approach to the provision of work.

The lone teleworkers are likely to be extremely loyal towards the organisation, partly because of the tremendous feeling of trust which is implied in this type of telework. Their employers are still likely, in the main, to be conventionally organised, and so the teleworkers may form only a small proportion of the total number of staff. This is probably the archetypal sort of teleworking which brings with it the benefits of employment and the flexibility of homework. To understand how it works, let us look at lone teleworking in two very different organisations.

COX PHARMACEUTICALS

Cox is a manufacturer of generic drugs, employing about 300 staff and turning over about £20 million per annum. It is now part of the Hoechst empire, and continues to run an efficient plant in Whiddon Valley, on the outskirts of Barnstaple in Devon.

The company's main business is in supplying retail pharmacists with a range of generic drugs, through a national sales and marketing operation. Regular contact with the pharmacists is necessary in this business, and in an attempt to ease the practical difficulties of regular calls to some of the more remote pharmacists, in 1982 the then sales manager, Colin Fearon took on two tele-salespeople to plug this gap. These were conventional office-based jobs, offered on a part-time basis, the main objective of which was to maintain contact with customers and take orders as and when required.

Judged to be a success from the customers' point of view, the arrangement soon began to cause a degree of internal strife. The salesmen in the field, nurtured on a regional competitiveness and measured against personal sales targets, viewed this imposition from head office with less than magnanimity, especially when any orders taken by telesales were swallowed up in the corporate finances, with no reflection on the regional basis.

By 1985 the situation was resolved: the tele-salespeople would work from a home base. They were given regional responsibility, and worked with small groupings of representatives in their own areas. There are now five in total, giving support and back-up to their areas. For example, where the calling frequency of the salesman is four weeks, this is interspersed with a call from the teleworker on a two-weekly basis. The arrangement is consolidated in such a way that the teleworker receives a percentage of the regional bonus.

A measure of how well the arrangement is working for Cox is evidenced by the fact that when covering for representatives on holiday, the telestaff average 66 per cent of the normal business for that area.

Selection

The regional sales managers each now have a teleworker in their regions, and are responsible for their recruitment in a process which is common to all staff at this level throughout the company. They have grown to expect a favourable interest from any recruitment activity for this type of work; a recent advertisement in a local paper which highlighted the teleworking theme produced 70 responses.

This in no way indicates that turnover is particularly high – 'about the same for sales staff as a whole'. Indeed, one of the original teleworkers from the early days of the scheme in Barnstaple has just reached retirement age. 'Other than ensuring the right skills in the applicant, there are no particular techniques we use,' says Colin Fearon, ' . . . the sales managers know what to look for. In the main they are loners, rather like the salespeople they support.'

The five regional teleworkers at Cox are all full-time employees with standard terms and conditions of employment for all staff at their grade within the company. No special allowances are made. Vacancies always generate interest from internal applicants, including male employees.

Equipment

The company insists on the teleworker being able to provide a dedicated space in which to work, though this need not be particularly large. The equipment requirement is limited to a business-specific phone line, a desk and the Telxon order-placing, messaging and paging system in use by the company. All the equipment is provided at the company's expense.

Work measurement

There are two expectations in terms of work measurement. First, staff are expected to be on call throughout the normal working day, in order to respond to enquiries from customers or their sales team – in other words, Cox is measuring a time-based input to work. Second, the work is results-orientated in that the teleworkers have a target call rate of 40 per day against which they are monitored.

Motivation

Many telesales operations, for example in the newspaper industry, rely heavily on the 'hype' that can be generated in telesales offices. So how does Cox deal with the potential for isolation within their scheme? Accepting the fact that careful selection probably leaves aside those with a high level of group communication needs, Colin Fearon is pragmatic about the need to provide the right motivation in the job, but does point out that in the main the telestaff are not 'cold calling'. Many of the pharmacists are regular clients: 'Most of the time, they're just ringing up old friends', he says.

But the organisation does much more to embrace the members into the team and address some of the social needs. The teleworkers are included on all relevant circulation lists; regional managers visit on not less than a monthly basis; the representatives are encouraged to make telephone contact whenever possible. Additionally, the teleworkers are invited to the annual national sales conference and the quarterly regional meetings.

For Cox Pharmaceuticals the practice works, and will be expanded as and when the business needs justify it, but their current experience demonstrates how a carefully organised scheme can provide the right support to the mainstream activity.

Let us now move on from Barnstaple to a much more extensive, and more recent, scheme – this time in the public sector. The London Borough of Enfield had vastly different motivations for their decision to teleorganise.

ENFIELD BOROUGH COUNCIL

The two key issues which led Peter James, the Finance Director, to recommend a teleworking scheme to elected members were the common organisational ailments of accommodation problems and recruitment difficulties. Being a large local authority, employing 10,000 people, the authority operates in a competitive employment market 'where general salary patterns lag behind the private sector'.

Peter James explained his dilemma. The administration of the community charge would create perhaps 60 or 70 new jobs, and he was determined to look at other alternatives to 'packing more and more people like sardines' into already fully utilised office space.

A home-based teleworking scheme was one of the options suggested by Stuart Dennison, the Assistant Director who heads the community charge division and is now developing and managing the programme. He explained: 'Some sort of cost justification was obviously important, but I would have still been pursuing the scheme, even if we hadn't been able to clearly show a cost saving.'

However attractive a social experiment this seemed to be, they had to demonstrate that the scheme carried with it no cost burden over conventional organisation. A realistic estimate by Peter James and Stuart Dennison of annual savings per head of £500 to £1,000 per annum, gained them the sanction to go ahead with the scheme.

At the outset there was one huge task to be completed – that of compiling the community charge register. Now, however, the range of tasks has become more diverse. The telework involves on-line access to the ICL mainframe at the Civic Centre, and a large proportion of the working day involves data input.

Selection and training

There is no shortage of applicants for the scheme. Local press advertising has produced good responses, the vast majority from women. Stuart Dennison explains how in practice selection and recruitment is operating.

> Quite often we are taking on people who have been out of the job market for maybe five to ten years. They are mainly carers, typically married women between 25 and 40. We're also looking at offering this as a career break opportunity for existing exployees.

Most of their recruits are new, not only to teleworking but also to local government and, interestingly, teleworkers do not need significant data processing experience. Stuart Dennison comments: 'We don't insist that they have had VDU experience, but we obviously expect basic keyboard skills, from typing or general clerical experience.'

What *is* insisted upon is that applicants are local: in practice that means living within 20 minutes' drive of the Civic Centre, as there is a great deal of transporting of documents in the scheme.

The selection interview is in two parts: a formal interview at head office, which includes aptitude tests, and then a visit to the potential teleworker's home for longer questioning about his or her working and domestic arrangements. Dennison always wants to see the room in which the teleworker proposes to work, to check out the location of phone points, the availability of natural light, and the general environment.

Once recruited, the teleworkers undergo personalised training programmes designed to help them to become up and running as full contributors. Their initial induction takes about two days, during which time they are introduced to the mechanics of the community charge, the department and the equipment.

The computer-based training module cannot be run on the home computers, and so there is always a mix of home-based training provided by the supervisors and more formal group sessions at the Civic Centre.

Dennison says: 'We got this right early on. It's in their contract that for training purposes they can be located other than at their homes. In reality it's probably 97 per cent at home, but it gives us the flexibility.'

Stuart Dennison also explains their means of accommodating the work style of their teleworkers: 'We do run the training sessions around the school runs, I wouldn't dream of suddenly putting in umpteen days of 9-to-5 training sessions for home-workers when many of them work from 9.00am to 3.30pm.'

In general the approach to training is to help to teleworkers to acquire task-specific skills, and to practise them extensively, before being invited back to the Head Office for further input. There is also specific training in data protection, comparable to that received by on-site staff but with specific attention paid to the added risks in the home-working environment.

Equipment and environment

A dedicated room is not a prerequisite, but Dennison does draw the line in instances: 'I don't expect a bedsit with about three people living in it, or anything approaching it. We don't want to transport the problems of crowded offices into the home environment.'

Teleworkers are provided with a second BT line so as to provide exclusive use with their dumb terminals. This allows continuous on-line computer access, as well as the ability to raise queries with their supervisor by phone.

Because most of the work requires on-line access for the majority of the working day, Enfield has opted to provide leased lines for the scheme, over which no time-based call charges are levied. However, whether these are across the switched network or leased, actually providing extra lines, certainly in residential areas, is not always straightforward. Dennison explains:

> BT have had great difficulty in some of the residential areas where they have basically run the wiring on the basis of one phone per house. We have had one or two occasions when this has taken several weeks, including digging up the road, before a line can be installed. So you have to have a fall-back, and that's usually the domestic phone.

In addition to the computer terminal, a desk and chair, teleworkers are provided with a lockable filing cabinet as part of the confidentiality requirement.

Work measurement and organisation

Once established, a teleworker will be expected to be capable of completing a menu of about a dozen tasks. Performance is monitored against the quantity of completed work.

Stuart Dennison makes broad comparisons with similar office-based jobs, but points out that in reality the tasks themselves are breaking new ground: 'For example, there is no equivalent office-based comparison for community charge registration, at least within this authority.'

However, he does believe that the potential for greater productivity is there because of a lower interruption factor: telephone calls, enquiries from other staff and from members of the public.

The proportion of work based at the VDU is 80–85 per cent, on-line to the mainframe. This imposes constraints on the flexibility of work that is allowed. Dennison points out: 'Teleworkers have a straight choice – any time they like between 28 and 36 hours within the 8.30am to 5.00pm day. But I do need to know in advance what people want to do.'

Management and motivation

The Enfield experience is that managers need a great commitment to their roles for success. It does not mean more of them, but certainly they are more visible and have to concentrate particularly on the planning and staff management aspects of their roles.

The telework supervisors, themselves home-based, maintain regular contact (usually three times a week) with their staff. Driven by the need to transport documentation, the payoffs are in the higher profile this gives them, and in the interdependence this creates in staff/supervisor relationships.

The supervisors, with Dennison, impose strict controls on the way work is carried out. Standards are high, and output monitored. This is partly the reason for the 'agreed hours' idea, which clearly attempts to divide working from non-working time in order to help the teleworker. But it also simplifies control and supervision. Dennison says:

> That's the reason for the agreed hours. The only people I would have going round outside those hours would be, say, furniture delivery people, and that would be by appointment. But routine machine maintenance, dropping off and collecting work, takes place within the agreed hours and obviously I would expect the teleworkers to be there. Obviously if they want a break for 15 minutes to do the school run, that's OK providing it's agreed and is not part of their hours. The supervisors need the flexibility to pop in at any time.

Though the work is largely focused on the VDU, the supervisors attempt to schedule the flow of work in order to allow breaks for other administrative duties, and the regular contact aids feedback from staff.

Isolation does not seem to be a major problem. Surprisingly, perhaps, when the work involves long stints of lone terminal operation. Dennison believes that one reason is that the telework is actually providing them with more outside contact than they had previously: the supervisory visits, telephone contact with colleagues, and group training sessions at the Civic Centre.

Teleworking develops interdependence, which spills over into social arrangements, and can be the catalyst which brings together near neighbours in a residential area. As Dennison remarks: 'Most of our people are not in the regular 9-to-5 office market, and as they look towards returning to work after a period of caring it's the nearest thing they can do to going back to the office, and it's often better.'

The scheme at Enfield is new, and the management techniques are developing on the basis of meeting needs through a practical approach. But what about appraisal, improved communications, social gatherings, career development and the like? Peter James and Stuart Dennison have their plans: 'Once we've got the scheme properly up and running, that's the time for those initiatives.'

Legal and administrative points

Standard contracts apply, except for the proviso that teleworkers must be prepared to travel to the Civic Centre for training purposes. However, there are guidelines about confidentiality and issues relating to data protection which are covered by the Data Protection Officer who makes visits to the teleworkers' homes.

A specific notice about Health and Safety is issued and draws attention to the dangers of trailing wires etc, especially where equipment is used in general working areas.

Use of rooms as business premises has not become an issue, because the average teleworker is relatively 'transparent', and many do not use rooms exclusively for their work. A sting in the tail for a local authority might be the need to collect from its teleworkers the uniform business rate, but the guidelines as they exist at present almost certainly do not embrace this type of telework. More of this, however, in Chapter 9.

Equipment insurance policies are not place-dependent and therefore cover the home-based sites.

Work reorganisation and productivity

A further problem with attempting to make direct comparisons between office-based and telebased work is that teleorganising has allowed the work to be distributed more effectively between office-based and telebased staff. In practise this means that the work carried out in the two environments is not the same.

Commitment to a high level of customer service had traditionally led office-based staff in the difficult, and sometimes depressing, position of attempting to resolve the competing claims of general administration, personal callers and phone calls. Staff had become quite used to 'desks full of stacks of paper' and were probably quite ingenious in coping with them.

Telework has brought about a change. As Peter James puts it, 'Staff may have gone home thinking, "Oh my God, I've got all these phone calls and all these personal callers as well – how am I going to deal with this big sack of paper?"'. The answer now is that in the main the teleworkers handle the big peaks in the programme. In other words productivity really takes off, with teleworking bringing benefits to office-based staff who see great piles of papers being distributed daily into the telenetwork.

This re-definition of tasks is yielding benefits in overall productivity, and freeing time for improved quality of service, from the department as a whole. Teleworking means that wherever staff are based, they can now become more effective in their work by being given a greater degree of control over their working day.

The boldness of scale and design of the Enfield project is already benefiting the department; as it gains in experience it will almost certainly become a model for other schemes.

4

The Teleoutposts

Once the idea of work provision becomes less of a mono-culture in employers' minds, and when the distance/cost relationship becomes less of an issue as telecoms costs tumble, 'harvesting' really can take off. This is the term used to describe the way in which organisations can reach out to, and benefit from the use of the vast pool of skills available in the community at large, rather than limiting work to that smaller population with the freedom, mobility or inclination to travel to work.

Why does claims processing or community charge administration require a fixed geographical base? This is a question which some organisations find difficult to answer, and traditional positions difficult to defend.

One way to harvest is by the use of the teleoutpost. These are not so much simply branch offices, which provide in the main a marketing function and therefore quite often a highly visible local profile; rather, teleoutposts are principally 'processing factories' located close to people in search of work. The location of the marketplace or the end user is often incidental. Typically work is transported to them, usually electronically, processed at the outpost and the results sent back to head office electronically.

This is a creative way of exploiting the falling cost gradient away from London, but also a way of social engineering in providing work, in work-poor areas. Organisations may have different motivations but, carefully designed, these schemes can lead to effective win/win situations, meeting the needs of employed and employer.

Note that the teleoutpost is based on grouping people together, and therefore facilitating the social contact that many people find necessary, thus having an appeal which outweighs some of the isolation problems which can affect the lone teleworker. It may also be much more comfortable for the employer, in that organisation and management there is likely to bear similarities to a conventional office setting: in other words, the teleoutpost for many is an acceptable way of allowing teleworking to come in from the cold.

A golden opportunity is afforded to those setting up teleoutposts, to challenge every convention and norm about office layout and working practise, and to export from head office only the culture and traditions that are of benefit—a green field opportunity.

So far, the new forms of work organisation that have been discussed are ancillary to the mainstream of activity. We have seen how organisations embrace the telehunters to take out the peaks and troughs, and how they foster the lone teleworkers in a symbiotic relationship. The two schemes which follow describe how teleoutposts have been successfully developed as another means of telework provision.

LLOYDS BANK

Initiatives in exploring alternative means of work provision are not new to Lloyds, but the motivators are such that by the mid-1990s the Bank will have devolved several thousand jobs from London.

They are pursuing two strategic objectives: first, to move people out of central London; second, to remove work itself from the capital. Gordon Edwards, who was the Regional Manager with responsibility for some of the initiatives, points to the two principal pressures for change: the all-too-familiar concerns of people and premises.

The rapid expansion of the Bank's business (they now have 115 branches in the London Region as a whole) was putting space at a premium, and at £60 per square foot this capital-based growth incurred high costs. People in London also have their price, and Lloyds were paying £3,200 London weighting for all staff at the beginning of 1990. This, combined with a staff turnover 2½ times greater than the Bank's national average, continues to make employing people in London a costly business.

Looking ahead throughout the 1990s, Lloyds sees the problems worsening, partly as a result of falling school rolls and the reality that the government is hoping to retain many of the Bank's target recruitment group (those with five or more GCSE passes at C or above) within the education system for longer.

In searching for ways to address this problem Lloyds realised that some of the creative ways of bridging the skills gap, which work in the provinces, are denied to businesses in central London. For example, because of the low resident population, schemes to attract women returners or older workers have been unsuccessful, partly because of the commuting time associated with travel from the suburbs. So, in heading up one of the initiatives in work devolvement, Gordon Edwards has managed the process of moving jobs from London – a process which, far from creating redundancies, has helped to ease the skills gap.

By the end of 1991 his aim is to have eight remote working centres up and running in the provinces which will take out 900 jobs from London. These are 'back office' jobs which require no personal customer contact. Of the eight projects, six will be work-processing centres where, for example, mortgage administration is controlled, and two will be devoted to word processing. The second of these will open in Scunthorpe next year, but one is already operational at Newton Aycliffe, employing about 110 staff.

This scheme developed from a project set up in Darlington in 1972, during an earlier typing crisis in the capital. It was a forerunner of the present scheme, but was for non-urgent work which was unaffected by the inevitable time lag involved in transport by overnight carrier services. Lloyds demonstrated its commitment to its staff by retaining the project in the area when the Darlington lease ran out, thus providing continuity of employment to those who wanted it. The new scheme was located at Newton Aycliffe and came into being in mid-1989.

Gordon Edwards describes the teleoutpost at Newton Aycliffe as 'essentially a typing factory', but anyone visiting it, or who saw the recent feature on BBC Television, will appreciate that this is far from being a 'dark satanic mill'. Careful thought and planning has resulted in an appealing and effective work environment.

The scheme provides an efficient word processing service to the 14 largest London branches, as well as five head office departments. The 110 word processing staff are handling the word processing requirements of up to 900 staff, or 'authors', in London at a striking rate. The remarkable standard of operation is that any work transmitted to Newton Aycliffe by 2.00pm will be on the desk of the author by 4.30pm.

Selection and training

One advertisement placed in three local newspapers produced a deluge of applications. Pay was a strong attraction; even shed of the London allowance, the national rate that Lloyds were offering in Newton Aycliffe was 25 per cent higher than the regional pay-rate in the north-east for word processing staff.

There are no special techniques or considerations to be made in selecting staff for this scheme. It is office based, and Lloyds' normal procedures apply. Most of the recruits into the scheme are new to banking. An induction course eases them into banking jargon, and they spend time at local branches to get some understanding of how the business operates. During 1990 it was planned to bring all the staff in groups down to London in order to meet the authors and establish some rapport with them.

Experience soon proved that as well as a training input at Newton Aycliffe, the London-based authors were also in need of training. They had already been dictating, but directly on to cassettes which were transcribed locally by their secretaries. Interposing 200 miles of electronic transmission, a change of accent, a very slight degradation in the quality of the message, and less knowledge of the dictating idiosyncracies of the authors, meant that problems at Newton Aycliffe were common. The solution was to improve the quality of dictation in London by running courses on a one-to-one basis, which is now occupying one of their training staff almost full-time. 'Would you like to hear what they heard you say at Newton Aycliffe last Tuesday?', seems to be typical of the approach which triggers off a big improvement in author dictation skills.

Equipment and environment

The Newton Aycliffe word processing centre is integrated into the Bank's voice and data nationwide communications networks. These are additional to links into the British Telecom and Mercury networks. Teleworkers can therefore make an immediate enquiry with the author in London about the tapes they are working on, as if they were in the next office.

The transmission system involves the tapes being played through 'sender boxes' in the branches into the private telecom network, and is word processed remotely before being transmitted back to the author's branch where the document is printed on the local laser printer. This system is a prime example of how processing work need not be place-dependent, provided that the telecoms structure, organisation and staff training are right.

When asked why they joined Lloyds Bank, the teleworkers said that they were attracted by the pay, with 'working conditions' as a close runner up. Lloyds have not cut costs in creating a pleasant airy working environment. They took outside advice and have produced working groups of four with sufficient space and greenery to break up the environment into comfortable working areas. Rest rooms, smoking and non-smoking areas, kitchens with microwaves and, recently, a hairdressing salon complement the facility.

Work measurement and productivity

Gordon Edwards explains what helps them to plan and monitor, and judge productivity against work in London.

> It might sound a bit mercenary, but we could actually measure productivity from London on the computer system. We actually know who are the most productive secretaries; we know the number of key strokes they do per hour or per minute.

So, is productivity higher? The answer is unequivocally yes, and for three reasons:

- a work-friendly environment;

- ease of acquiring more able staff, who stay longer and contribute more;

- job design dedicated to word processing, which cuts out conventional office interruptions.

In addition to measures of individual performance, output standards are set such as the deadlines for the turnaround of work.

Management and motivation

The management structure is conventional, though of course Newton Aycliffe is a part of London Region. A great deal of care is put into the selection of the supervisory staff within the scheme, and the manager in particular has a much higher personnel profile to his or her role – partly because of the remoteness from London staff, and central support.

At present, all staff work full-time and are organised into three units of 36 each with an assistant. The word processor operators are divided into teams of four. This is a user-friendly arrangement aimed at increasing the identity between authors and their operators. So, for example, if someone in the Stock Exchange branch sent work to Newton Aycliffe, it would be directed to one of the three units. It should be handled on a regular basis by a specific team of four within a unit.

Gordon Edwards is satisfied that they have created a classically 'hygienic' work environment, and believes that the two prime motivators of pay and working conditions are probably extending their motivational 'honeymoon period'. It may be enough, but already he is thinking of ways to anticipate motivational problems. Part-time working and flexible shifts may be part of the solution for the future, to further improve the output of the centre.

However, these concerns for the future in no way undermine the current success of the scheme. Applicants are in the wings waiting for jobs which may appear through growth but not often by staff turnover, which is 1 per cent at present – well below the local norm of about 6 per cent. Lloyds expect the figure to rise, but this norm is a useful benchmark against which to gauge the success of their own scheme.

Legal and contractual issues

Because the work is office-based and the teleworkers are retained on standard terms and conditions comparable to others at their grades in the Bank, there are no issues specific to the remote working units.

For the final summary on the Lloyds experience to date, Gordon Edwards comments:

> In three years' time we will have a much better idea of the success of the project. We know already that it is a financial success, with the anticipated cost savings being captured. It is a 99 per cent technical success, though we'll have to keep up with technological developments. From the people viewpoint we are very pleased with the start we have made, but I am pragmatic and wary about making predictions for the future.

THE ROYAL BOROUGH OF WINDSOR AND MAIDENHEAD

Mike Kirby, Data Processing Manager of the Royal Borough of Windsor and Maidenhead, says: 'Windsor and Maidenhead is not a normal local authority; quite simply, it's the best in the country'.

No doubt many would challenge this assertion as a matter of fact, but few could question Mike Kirby's enthusiasm for the data processing function and the quality of service offered to the 250 or so end users within the authority.

With a population of fewer than 150,000 spread over 76 square miles, the Royal Borough of Windsor and Maidenhead is typical of many Shire District authorities, which have had to cope with considerable change in their procedures throughout the 1980s.

Geoffrey Blacker, Chief Executive and Borough Treasurer, was the driving force behind the authority's total re-evaluation of its approach to information technology, which was managed through to completion by Mike Kirby. Following a thorough review in 1984, the authority followed the IBM route and installed a 4381 processor along with IBM Database 2 (DB2) software.

Coupled with the introduction of the new equipment came a demand for trained DB2 professionals, to meet the expansion of information technology applications within the authority. The computer department headcount needed to grow from 13 to about 23. Recruitment and retention became a real issue.

Mike Kirby became only too well aware of the marketability of his DB2-trained staff when in 1987 he had nine vacancies out of a total establishment of twelve in the development section. Home-growing DB2 professionals was a slow process and he was forced into the costly alternative of contract support, which helped neither morale in the department, nor the budget.

Yet again, difficulties in recruitment and retention of staff had forced an organisation to look down the teleroute. Geoffrey Blacker saw this as an opportunity not only to help with the skills shortage, but also as a means of breaking down the 'north-south' divide, which had become a prominent issue at the time.

Although they were a Tory-controlled authority they were looking to target an area of high unemployment, which meant that the eventual 'partner' was likely to be a Labour authority of similar size and probably north of Watford.

Three years after the initial search Mike Kirby now has an efficiently run teleoutpost in Telford employing 5 of his total computing staff of 23. Mike is a pragmatist, and views the success of the project partly in terms of the way it has been received by those in the organisation, who are not themselves directly involved in telework. He comments: 'In fact there is not one person in this computer section who would tell you that the remote unit was a bad idea, partly because they have seen the calibre of the people up there.'

Mike Kirby operates four business units, technical support, development, operations and, at Telford, the remote development unit, describing their work as 'fairly typical local authority: payroll, rates, rents, community charge, housing benefits and internal financial management.'

Selection and training

The original local press advertising campaign highlighted the remote working angle, but produced a disappointing response. Most of the original positions were filled via recruitment agencies. Specific training in DB2 was necessary, but because of the outpost nature of the operation, which is essentially a branch office, none was needed in the specific aspect of how to be a teleworker.

Management and motivation

Mike Kirby has tried to export his normal managing culture from Maidenhead to Telford, and says: 'I don't set deadlines, I just point to windows and encourage staff to take a look through, and encourage them to get themselves to the other side of the project.'

Staff have a great degree of control over the structure of their working day. Being largely project-based the work is mainly proactive. Flexitime operates, but whereas there is a time-clock recording system for staff at the head office, Mike relies on a different mechanism for those at Telford: 'They are 150 miles away. That means you have got to trust your staff.'

Performance-related pay was introduced in 1988 which has helped in lifting the rewards in the section to within the top third of employers using IBM software. An appraisal scheme allows scope for a reward-based bonus scheme, which the business unit heads can allocate within their sections, including the remote development unit at Telford.

From the outset Mike Kirby has been aware of the potential for isolation within the unit. He remarks: 'We set various rules early on because we were conscious of the contact point of view. We wanted them to feel part of the computer section, not just a bolt-on extra.' This commitment to involvement is taken seriously. The Chief Executive and several elected members were present at the launch. The computer development working group, comprising elected members and senior officers, meets six times per year and once at Telford, where, following the business meeting, the staff from the unit are invited along socially.

The main progress meeting of the month, which again usually involves all the Telford staff, is held at a 'half-way house' in Moreton-in-the-Marsh, where they meet with Mike Kirby, any other relevant section heads and their client groups.

Mike Kirby believes that this commitment to involvement, clearly set and attainable goals, and a credible reward system provide the key to a satisfactory base of morale and motivation. He describes the time he spends at Telford as being, 'rather more than you might expect for purely business reasons', in that he is eager to keep in touch with the sentiments of those at Telford.

Legal and contractual issues

In contractual terms, Telford is merely an office remote from the head office. All staff are full-time employees of the authority with appropriate terms and conditions of employment.

Equipment

The original 9.6 kilostream link between the teleoutpost and the authority's main offices has now been upgraded to 48 kilostream. This now allows all the staff there to work on-line to the mainframe. Fax, electronic mail and 'a multitude of printers' mean that there is very little reliance on postal or courier systems.

Because Mike Kirby meets at least monthly with the unit head at Telford, this forms the usual means by which pay slips, expense claims and other documentation is transferred.

Work measurement and output

Strict performance measures are in place by the setting of agreed project target dates. Monitoring of individual performance is by the appraisal system.

Projects are exchanged between the main computer section and Telford, which helps to maintain cohesion but makes any comparison of productivity between the two units very difficult. In any event there appears to be no reason why productivity should differ. Mike Kirby says: 'They're all basically in offices; it's their own individual motivation and the way I do my job which makes the difference.' His experience demonstrates how teleoutposts can be effective ways of teleworking, and that to be successful these do not have to be large schemes.

The track records in the last two chapters illustrate different approaches to teleorganising. However, in all of them one essential ingredient rests with the parent organisation – that is, the control and provision of work.

But a new era of teleprovision is now with us, allowing new opportunities to be exploited. We look at some of these in the next chapter.

5
The Teleco-ops

Teleco-ops exploit both the cost gradient from the south-east and the geographically dispersed skills pool, into a marketable package which can be sold to organisations in the major conurbations. They are a means of bringing together a range of skills and presenting them in a package to distant users.

They differ from teleoutposts in several respects. First, control rests with the owners of the teleco-ops, acting as the body which marshalls the various skills of individuals within a locality. Second, the contracting organisation has no involvement in the teleco-op other than a concern for delivery of results, normally enshrined in the contractual arrangement between the two. For the user organisation, this is a means of subcontracting, but the advantage over more traditional forms may be that the teleco-op takes on board much of the administration associated with the contract.

The three schemes which follow are relatively new, and developing. It is not possible to judge their long-term success, but each is making a positive beginning.

THE FRONTLINE INITIATIVE

In July 1988 the National Economic Development Office (NEDO) with its co-sponsors the Department of Trade and Industry, the Confederation of Information and Communication Industries, and 15 commercial sponsors, commissioned a report to explore the question: Could the advances in computer and telecoms technology be utilised cost-effectively in taking IT-based work to areas of high unemployment in the inner cities?

The feasibility study, Project Frontline, was completed in December that year, and as a result of the report to the sponsors, the Frontline Initiative was launched. Part of the initiative involved the setting up of a charitable trust which exists to encourage and support ways in which information technology can be applied to achieve worthwhile economic and social benefits.

The other part of the Frontline Initiative is about social engineering using telework to profitable ends. Horace Mitchell, a director of

Frontline Initiative is pooling private sector and government money in a drive to provide an inner-city solution to unemployment, by marketing the IT skills of people in the north to the hungry businesses of the south.

The initiative is setting up five centres in inner-city areas, geared to undertaking a variety of information technology and related tasks. Completed work will then be transferred electronically back to the buyers of the service in the south.

Figure 5.1 shows the proposed regional centres, the London marketing centre, and the sort of staffing level envisaged in each. The first centre, in Nottingham, opened its doors for business on 29 May 1990.

This is not at the outset a straight commercial venture, and when you look at the Frontline strategy, you can see why this is so:

- They are locating in unattractive areas that have recognised infrastructure and employment problems;

- They recruit among the unemployed and the inexperienced;

- They seek to identify aptitude and talent, and train so as to optimise potential rather than to meet a pre-conceived business need.

Normal market forces would probably not steer a purely commercial organisation down this route. The plight of the inner cities is due in large part to the decline of their traditional industries, making them unattractive for the new IT-based sunrise industries. The Frontline Initiative realises that a purely commercial approach might lead it to target Maidstone rather than Moss Side.

Equally, IT companies are more likely to seek out experienced people rather than trainees, and qualified graduates rather than those with mere potential. Again commercial pressures would lead an organisation to areas already strong in computing talent or IT Departments of universities and polytechnics.

But Project Frontline is not mere charity or philanthropy, Horace Mitchell is clear about their goals; he says: 'This is big strategic investment with a delayed pay-off rather than the minimal tactical outlay with the earliest possible recovery.' Nevertheless he sees a truly commercial profit-based organisation within three years. There seems little doubt that the market is there, and by bridging the north-south divide, telework will allow Frontline to deliver the goods.

Business structure

The term 'co-op' is not entirely accurate, but certainly the Frontline Initiative has a collective theme to its organisation. The management is currently in search of 20 or so client firms to take a stake in the business.

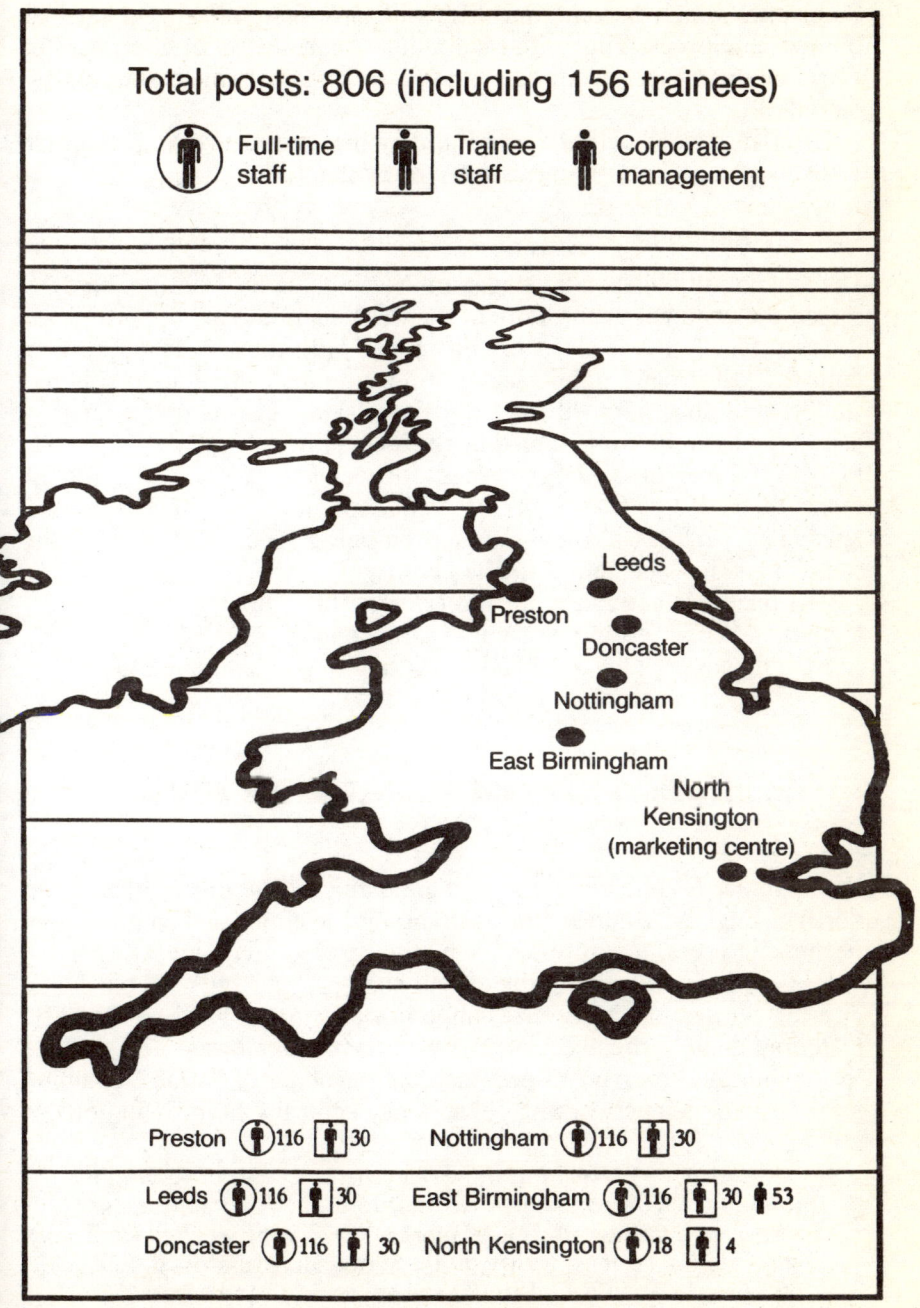

Figure 5.1 The Frontline Initiative: locations and staffing

Companies which become members will have first call on the pool of trained employees. The initial stake for companies is of the order of £150,000 guaranteeing a programme of work against which staff can be recruited.

The Department of Trade and Industry has agreed to match the first £300,000 raised from the private sector by grant aid.

Local recruitment

The community liaison manager in Nottingham is working hard to spread the word about the work of the Centre and the job opportunities it offers. The Centre is also working actively with those in IT training in both the private and public sectors to ensure a steady flow of suitable staff into the business with the right core skills. In this way it supplements the basic training offered by the local providers and develops staff for the IT market at large. When the scheme is fully operational Frontline estimates that it will be producing probably 150 well-trained 'graduates' per year, already with substantial experience of working for some of the top companies in the country.

It is relatively early days for Project Frontline, but the scheme is on target and is one of the most ambitious examples yet of how to use the converging power of telecoms and computing to generate new and flexible ways of providing work.

THE UK TELENETWORKING INITIATIVE FOR RURAL AREAS

What Horace Mitchell and his team are doing for the inner cities of the north of England, Andrew Page is doing for the more rural communities of the south-west and, prospectively, the north of Scotland.

He is actively developing the idea of business exchanges which act as clearing houses for the diverse range of skills in the local community, matching them to the needs of local and distant employers. He describes the first business exchange, operating from the offices of Protocol Communications, the telenetworking consultancy company he runs in Totnes:

> . . . a laboratory, exploring the development of ways of turning a town into a 'telecommunity'. We want to use telecommunications services and facilities to help to support local life, by securing work and fostering business activity in the surrounding rural areas. And, of course, location is no barrier to where services can be marketed.

The initiative is gaining much support and interest from other parties with a stake in rural development, and Andrew Page is shepherding this interest from local authorities, British Telecom, the Training Agency, and Business in the Community (BIC) towards the establishing of business exchanges throughout rural areas generally. Following the pioneer project in Totnes, Prince Charles is actively supporting the idea through BIC, and Francis Kinsman, the well-respected futurist and teleconsultant, is acting as an adviser to the schemes.

Andrew Page defines the initiative as encompassing teleworking, teletraining, and other activities: for example telebanking, teleshopping, and other activities which can be conducted on a location-independent basis via telecoms links.

Suitably packaged, it is easy to see why employers might be interested in the business exchanges. Once again this is a project which allows them access to skills which are in short supply, without the associated on-cost of heavy overheads, and inflated pay rates.

But there are desirable benefits to the local regions too in stabilising employment, especially for the young. Such telework will bring employment into rural areas, enabling the local population to work at home or in the locality rather than having to move away. Similarly, with an increase in the amount of work being delivered electronically to the people, rather than vice versa, traffic congestion should be eased. As Andrew Page points out:

> We think this is particularly appropriate for rural areas. We feel that
> it would be advantageous for urban firms to use telecommuters. The
> new type of working is suited to the rural environment of the region
> and will benefit employers as well as the resident population.

But what do the business exchanges have to offer? In short, a range of physical, technological and social support mechanisms to those wishing to trade their skills to others at the exchange. Figure 5.2 overleaf outlines the sort of support services which will help the individual benefit from the collective umbrella of the business exchange. They are detailed below.

1. Community Information Centre: a walk-in information service linking the enquirer to citizen and consumer information and advisory services, small business advisory services, grant-aiding organisations etc. This could also serve as a Telecommuter Employment Bureau.
2. The telemarket: a range of 'market stalls' sharing access to on-line product catalogues. Help would be provided for tele-shoppers, so as to enable them to make the best use of the services and products offered by distant retailers. A teleconferencing link would allow local business people to make presentations to distant buyers.

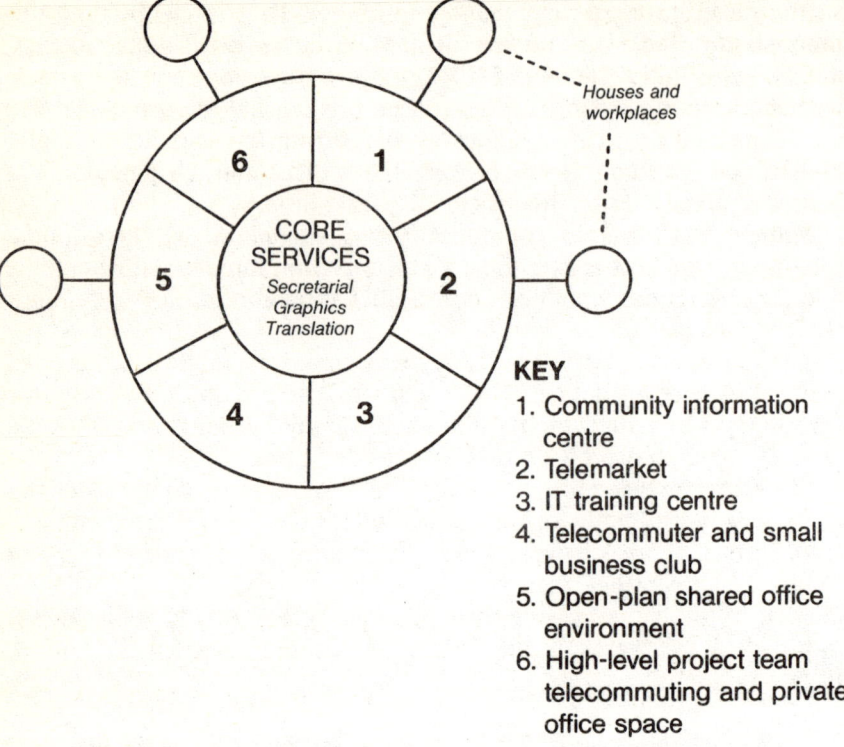

Houses and
workplaces

KEY
1. Community information
   centre
2. Telemarket
3. IT training centre
4. Telecommuter and small
   business club
5. Open-plan shared office
   environment
6. High-level project team
   telecommuting and private
   office space

Figure 5.2 Modular elements of Business Exchange

3. IT training centre: probably in collaboration with local schools and other training providers to ensure ongoing IT training for businesses and telecommuters.
4. Telecommuter and small business club: an opportunity for social and professional interaction for telecommuters who need to escape the potential isolation of home-work. Small conference rooms and a video conferencing suite would complete the range of services.
5. Open-plan shared environment: this will allow individuals to 'rent a desk' on flexible terms.
6. High-level project team facility: secure private office space with high-quality computing facilities to provide sophisticated support for company project teams and individuals.

Both this project and the Frontline Initiative are by their nature long-term investments, involving the need to educate and reorientate the views of those in search of scarce skills and those who have them on offer. Wide collaboration is necessary for such projects to thrive.

Andrew Page tested the market for his ideas at an early stage by launching a pilot Skills Register in the Totnes area, among individuals as well as businesses. He wanted to gauge the potential of finding people with the appropriate skills for telecommuting, and after more than 1,000 applicants and strong indications of interest from three major employers he is convinced that the project is on course. The pilot, he confirms, 'has been completely satisfactory from all points of view'.

Most recently the EC Commission has commissioned Protocol to investigate teleworking and to formulate recommendations on how teleworking issues should be addressed in possible future EC actions.

TELECOTTAGES INTERNATIONAL

Vemdalen, a remote village in the north of Sweden, became the site of the first telecottage in September 1985. Traditional sources of employment were in decline, and it took the vision of Henning Albrechtsen with the support of the Swedish authorities and telephone company to establish the pilot telecottage with £100,000-worth of computers and telecommunications facilities.

Deemed a success, with 40 per cent of the population using the facility, similar telecottages were soon developed throughout Scandinavia, leading to the development of the Nordic Association of Telecottages FILIN, representing about 50 telecottages.

Until recently, Ashley Dobbs was the UK honorary representative of Telecottages International (TCI). Established in 1988 as a non-government, non-profit making organisation, the aim of TCI is to spread the experience of running telecottages around the world and to create a 'network of intelligence' where telecottages can 'swap' intelligence: for example, one telecottage could translate English into Japanese, and another might typeset a magazine.

The first UK telecottage was opened in December 1989 at the Manifold County Primary School in Buxton, Derbyshire. This supports a creche and a canteen, in addition to telecoms and computing equipment. British Telecom, the local Education Authority and the Rural Development Commission have been active in funding, and indeed BT is considering funding a position for a full-time adviser to the telecottage concept.

What is a telecottage?

Essentially it is a room in a village, which is available to local people for learning or work, creating revenue and employment through, for example, computer training, desktop publishing, distance learning, business planning, accountancy or word processing and translation.

TELEWORKING

There are two main categories of telecottage, the first being community telecottages, providing a range of services on a non-profit making basis. They tend to supplement and benefit the local community by providing IT help for local businesses, or indeed the farming community. For example, farmers in Fjalting in north-west Jutland attend training in computing and use specialist software to plan their farming activities. The second type is the business telecottage which in many ways resembles the city or town-based service office or business bureau, with central secretarial services.

The development of telecottages is unlikely to be a centrally coordinated activity, depending rather on the enthusiasm and drive of key individuals throughout the various rural communities probably investing their own funds in the main, but also in search of help from the various authorities which may express an interest and support the development of information-based work in rural areas. For example, the Highlands and Islands Development Board, the Welsh Development Agency, and the EC in the form of ORA (Opportunities for Applications of Information Technology and Telecommunications in Rural Areas) are all active in evaluating suitable forms of remote working including telecottages.

British Telecom have promoted the idea of remote work quite extensively through advertising campaigns and other intiatives, although it is unlikely that their support will lead to an extensive involvement in telecottages, beyond perhaps several pilot projects.

6

The Teleorganisations

There are two sub-species within this group, with implications for internal organisation and the way in which they market their services.

First there are the companies 'without offices', or so the media would have us believe. CPS and the FI Group are the most often quoted and in reality embrace a mixture of the teleforms which have been discussed in earlier chapters. Lone teleworking, and developments around the outpost or workcentre theme, are all methods incorporated by these organisations. They operate in the computer software consulting field, and in information technology in general. What characterises them is better management, a flexible approach to the provision of work, and a healthy dislike of too many offices. Most of their staff are home-based and provide support services to clients operating in their locality.

What differentiates the second type of teleorganisation from those such as FI is the geography of the relationship between the client and the company. In the first group, telemanaging allows the organisation to offer its skills on a local basis to end users – in other words the telecoms infrastructure is primarily an internal method of communication. In the latter group, the main business is the processing of data from a fixed site, using telecoms as both the distribution and delivery vehicle. BIS Beecom in Ireland is an example of this type of organisation, able to conduct its business internationally by telecoms link.

This chapter deals with perhaps the best known and longest running teleschemes, which fall into this first category.

CPS PROFESSIONAL SERVICES

CPS is one of two remote working divisions of International Computers (ICL) which has recently been bought from STC by Fujitsu. There are now about 250 staff, the great majority of whom are home-based teleworkers, providing a range of integrated solutions to meet the information technology needs of specific markets, within ICL and to third party users.

The group was started as a six-month trial in 1969 when a manager within ICL grasped an opportunity to solve the problem of a shortage of good programming resources. He phoned one of his staff, who had left the previous year to have a baby, and sold the idea of resourcing the project from a home-working base. A team of ten similarly placed ex-employees soon formed the core of what has grown over the years to become CPS – a well-respected organisation in its field. Incidentally, the first CPS teleworker, Hilary Cropper, is now Chief Executive of the FI Group, the other pioneer in UK teleorganisation.

Throughout the 1970s and 1980s CPS continued to grow, employing analysts, designers, programmers, technical authors, project managers and consultants. In 1984, the newly appointed Divisional Director commissioned a consultants' report of the organisation which led to the drafting of a mission statement for the group as follows:

> To be the preferred supplier of its professional services to end users in our chosen markets, and a high technology showcase for home-based computer professionals; to continue to provide high calibre development and author resources to ICL's business centres.

A new development for CPS is their remote working consultancy headed by Sue Halbert, which provides help to organisations investigating telework schemes. CPS is also collaborating with IT World and the CBI in the preparation of a report, to be called 'The impact of Teleworking in the 1990s'.

Selection and training

There is a waiting list to get into CPS. In 1989 they received nearly 1,000 applicants for about 60 vacancies. Exposure in trade journals and whispers on the professional grapevine ensure a steady stream of applicants. Is there a typical applicant profile? Sue Halbert explains:

> About 50 per cent of our staff come from within ICL, the rest from competitors or end users. About 10 per cent of the total are men, and I don't expect that to change much. Interestingly, the age profile is increasing to between about 30 to 45. I suppose the population of computer-literate people in that age group has grown tremendously.

A minimum of five years' previous and relevant experience is also required, and this is reflected within CPS where the average level of experience is about 14 years. The selection procedure also searches out the applicants' self-discipline, initiative as problem solvers, their flexibility, and their ability to communicate, particularly over the telephone which is perhaps the most available means to them.

Other prerequisites are a suitable dedicated work space at home. Part of the interview procedure is to establish precisely where the potential teleworker will work. Sue Halbert comments: 'Yes, we always ask them where they are going to work. If the answer is the kitchen table, we know it won't work. They need a dedicated space, somewhere that is private and quiet.'

Interviews are normally held at an ICL office, as the ability to travel to one is simply part of the job. Most applicants have cars and driving licences, which are necessary for visits to site and client premises.

Low turnover has been a reflection of the quality of the recruitment process, but this has been increasing over the last year, probably for two reasons, as Sue Halbert explains:

> First of all, there is now a market for teleworkers. Five years ago if you wanted to be a teleworker you went to FI or ourselves; now there is a lot more choice. Second, because of our structure, recruiting is now delegated down the line, and perhaps we need to better prepare people for this responsibility. We looked recently at ways of tackling this issue.

One of the key points in the interviewing process, as well as looking at the level of technical competence of the applicants, is to explore their motivations in considering telework. A major motivation is the need to combine working with caring, and as a result many teleworkers are part-time, with working hours ranging from 16 to 37 per week, with an average of about 21.

On appointment all new teleworkers are assigned to a mentor, probably living locally, who can help them to make the transition into becoming effective teleworkers. Ongoing training is available to CPS staff as in the rest of ICL, though the particular difficulties of their working arrangements are acknowledged. Distance-learning packages are used, and bearing in mind that many staff are part-time workers with commitments that may involve complicated logistics with child minders and school runs, standard five-day training programmes are usually presented in shorter modules.

Training for managers is comprehensive, particularly to enable them to understand the motivational needs of off-site staff, but as Sue Halbert contends, 'All we try to instil is basically good management technique, but more of it, so we try to emphasise their role in developing individuals.'

Management structure and organisation

CPS has always attempted to modify its management structure to meet both its internal needs and business opportunities. For members of staff not yet part of the management, the structure was likely to have several reporting lines, which had been leading to some confusion. This was rectified by the appointment of team leaders about 18 months ago, which introduced another tier into the management structure. As Sue Halbert explains:

> These are, if you like, the working staff managers. Reporting to them is a team put together on a geographical basis. They deal with 'pay and rations', passing on of information and general communications. Importantly they are the source of continuity, and for this reason carry out appraisals. We introduced them to try to overcome an isolation problem which until then resulted from the fact that staff were drifting around, working for two or three months with one project manager and then moving on to another for a further six months.

Team leaders report to area managers, and through regional managers to the general manager, Diana Hill, in addition to marketing, technical, and new business managers.

All the staff and managers are home-based, the managers having local secretarial support, with secretaries coming into their homes for mostly 10 to 12 hours per week. The senior tier of managers are all full-time.

Administrative support is provided by two small technical offices in Kidsgrove and Bracknell, employing five people in all.

Although CPS staff collaborate closely with conventionally-based colleagues in other parts of the company, management recognised early on that a separate structure was necessary in order to prevent the home-workers being seen as an adjunct to the main business.

For Sue Halbert the fundamental management style must be management by output. For CPS this normally means meeting project deadlines. She cites the design and implementation of a course booking system as an example project, which was completed on schedule within four months. The project team was made up of a systems designer from Glasgow, a programmer based in Harrow, and a technical author based in Carmarthen. Careful coordination and monitoring of progress by the project manager meant that the system was delivered on time. Incidentally, for this project the team never actually met face to face.

Motivation

At one period in their development, when about 40 people were employed, the reporting line was changed such that the teleworkers had an on-site manager as their boss. They were split into teams and fragmented throughout the organisation. There was a consequent fall in morale and sense of involvement, accompanied by the belief that the teleworkers were regarded as a bolt-on accessory to the main unit, absorbing the less creative work and managed by a boss who did not understand what it was like to be a teleworker. As a result, staff drifted out of the organisation.

The current structure, clearly identified as a teleworking unit, has helped to restore morale and lift the identity and image of CPS. The moral of the story is to clearly identify the teleworking groups, make the managers teleworkers, and design systems which do not conflict with the special emphasis of remote management. Part of the process of formalising the structure of CPS has been to raise the status of its employees. Sue Halbert explains: 'We are very conscious, particularly these days, that people are working for us not as a hobby, and not just to earn a bit of money before the start of a holiday. They are working because they actually need the money.'

Although many of them are part-time workers, the challenge of management is to maintain a workflow which yields high productivity, without having to interfere with the agreed working hours of members of staff. Sue Halbert continues: 'If they are going to dedicate themselves to a certain number of hours per week, they may have regular child-minding commitments. You can't expect them to switch on and off their child minders to suit the whims of the contractor.'

CPS works hard to respond to feedback from its staff. Part of the reason for appointing team leaders was the feedback from the regular staff newsletters which indicated that 'social isolation' was a problem for many. Site visits to clients within ICL or outside are one practical way in which this problem is tackled, the frequency varying between once per month and four times per week. In practice this means that staff are *based* at home rather than working exclusively at home.

CPS believes that it addresses these problems by its dedication to management by output, its management style tuned to telework, and a structure which helps to develop a community of teleworkers. Sue Halbert is clear about why this should be: 'You can build up a good team spirit by remote working, provided that you accept that dependence within the team is probably greater.'

Legal and contractual issues

CPS staff are full employees of ICL. They benefit from the same terms and conditions and pay of their office-based counterparts. Where appropriate these are scaled down on a *pro rata* basis to the hours they work. All expenses are paid including travelling time from their homes. They also benefit from a contributory pension scheme.

The whole package has developed from the *ad hoc* arrangement in the mid-1970s when teleworkers simply invoiced the organisation for the time they spent working. The attention of the auditors and the Inland Revenue took the view that as they were working exclusively for ICL they were in fact employed by them, which started the trend of bringing them into the fold of true employment.

By abolishing the differences between office-based and home-based staff, CPS has been able to create a motivated work unit that has developed its own credibility within the organisation.

Equipment and environment

Technical staff have powerful micros; the managers have personal computers. They can be linked via the public switched network. Electronic mail is in general use as are answer machines, which have proved to be a great boon in reducing time wastage and frustration when colleagues are trying to liaise on a project. Faxes are not part of the routine equipment at present, but may be included as the cost falls.

Work measurement and productivity

Management processes at CPS focus on tight control, formalised planning, scheduling, regular project review, and the maintenance of appropriate standards of performance. The concern is with output and, although pay is based on hours worked, performance is monitored during the appraisal process.

The strategy for success at CPS stems from the implementation of four key elements:

- Top-level commitment;
- Selecting the right jobs and the right staff;
- Well equipped and well trained staff;
- Strong management.

THE FI GROUP

No account of teleworking can ignore the remarkable story of the energy and persistence of Steve Shirley, the founder of probably the largest and most documented teleorganisation. Since its inception in 1962 and through several metamorphoses, the FI Group now ranks in the top 20 software houses in Britain. From the outset the company has been distinguished from its competitors by its method of incorporating self-employed staff as 'panel members'.

Steve Shirley's 'original act of creation' was to persuade office managers, chief executives and departmental heads that they were not getting the personal attention they needed from their hardware suppliers. At the same time she was painfully aware of the loss from the industry, already suffering from a chronic skill shortage, of women who 'could not reconcile the conflicting desire to rear their own children with the demands of a vigorous career.'

The alchemy that Steve Shirley worked, against all the odds, was to merge the planning of human resources, premises and automation to offer an unrivalled service to clients. To do this she had to bring together highly skilled people from all over the country within one nationwide company.

The company now has around 800 staff, roughly 75 per cent of them being self-employed. Steve Shirley's initial instinct, that there were far more female IT professionals with a desire to combine work with raising children than conventional employers were prepared to take on, is still largely borne out by the current staff complement.

Clearly FI is something of a haven for those with the right ability, and conviction, which is a fundamental tenet of their mission: 'To develop, through modern telecommunications, the unutilised intellectual energy of people unable to work in a conventional environment'.

There are many similarities between FI and CPS, and this short account seeks to highlight the differences between them rather than to mirror those things that they share in common.

Selection and training

From a steady stream of unsolicited applicants, FI select 'those most likely to enjoy keeping us a leader in the systems business'. Getting into the selection procedure requires:

- four years' experience and/or suitable qualifications;
- the ability to do at least 20–25 productive hours per week during a project;
- the ability to undertake two or more local client visits per week, child-minding arrangements being made accordingly where necessary;
- a telephone and some kind of 'office area' at home;
- own transport or easy access to public transport;
- high standards of professionalism and self-discipline.

The business of incorporating diverse backgrounds and skills into the FI culture is largely a matter of training. Steve Shirley offers pragmatic advice: 'If you are thinking of adding value to your own products and services, I recommend training as a quality add-on. In FI Group each line manager is a trainer. And all of us go on courses as well as give them.'

All staff are considered for career development opportunities, and training in technical and management skills is carried out by a variety of methods. All their programmes are geared to individual and business needs and are delivered through a variety of methods: computer-based, open or distance learning, and the use of in-house and public training events.

Management structure and organisation

The management structure is similar to that in more orthodox organisations but with an important difference: that is, the arm's-length working arrangement. Effectively FI has replaced the office routine with a flexible structure of communication, often electronically and by telephone, by post and in person. That is the fundamental difference, which stems from Steve Shirley's orientation to their business. She says: 'I challenge the conventional financial statement which quotes buildings as an asset and the cost of people as an expense, because to us it is people who are the asset and the buildings which are the expense.'

As the business has grown, internal restructurings have reshaped the organisation, from a production orientated, regionally organised one into one which is technology and marketing orientated, with a national sales force. The need to change perhaps resulted from the dispersed nature of the business, but is in itself a re-focus which is not limited to teleorganisation.

Motivation

Steve Shirley believes there are two things which will improve people's performance, namely motivation and training. FI attempts to listen to its workforce. The monthly 'Freespeaks' were a result of this, and allow a much more open forum for communications.

Perhaps the prime motivator for many of the staff is the ability to choose and design their own career structure, combining it with raising a family if they so choose, and to be taken seriously, particularly in the first of these roles. Creating an environment in which that can happen is a hallmark of FI, where Steve Shirley believes that: 'Our networkers enjoy mental gymnastics and are perhaps a new breed, able to adapt and thrive on independence and the challenge of working in new ways.'

Legal and contractual issues

Most of FI staff are self-employed, accounting for about 75 per cent of the total. They operate as members of the home-based 'panel', and are engaged to provide services in connection with specific contracts.

As will be seen in a later chapter the law, in the form of the various statutory bodies such as the Inland Revenue and Customs and Excise, attempts to differentiate between the employed and self-employed status. Therefore, in attempting to preserve the independence of its panel as self-employed staff, FI has to take care in extending the corporate hand of involvement.

In practice the particular work methods of the FI Group have formed test cases in determining just what is and what is not self-employment. So, for a self-employed panel member of FI there is no sick pay, holiday pay or superannuation. They are liable for VAT if their turnover dictates it.

FI personal accident cover extends to panel members at work, as does equipment cover for any of the Group's equipment at panel members' homes.

Equipment and environment

Rather surprisingly, the FI Group has achieved its current position largely on the drive of its people, with only a little technological help. The personal computer and the telephone have been the mainstays of the growth phase.

The company is now moving on rapidly towards developing its combined network. Interestingly, as well as incorporating leased lines into major client businesses, and linking up all managers and company offices with electronic mail, the group now has a small network of five workcentres, which are distinct from mere offices in that they operate purely as business units, providing facilities only for teams of analysts and programmers, working directly on customer projects – lean, productive and profitable are the key words in work centres.

Work measurement and productivity

Productivity within the panel is significantly higher than in office-based environments. The key to high productivity is monitoring and a careful breakdown into project stages with definable goals to be achieved in a minimum number of hours. The participative culture at FI helps to underpin this high level of output.

These accounts of teleworking in their various forms are intended to demonstrate that teleworking in one shape or another is within reach of many organisations and, probably, of sections or functions of all organisations.

Part II: Key Point Summary

- There are many forms of telework, other than the common notion of home teleworking. It is primarily concerned with the collection, processing and distribution of information and services which may not be place-dependent. A simple classification includes the work environments and habits of lone teleworkers, teleoutposts, teleco-ops and teleorganisations.

- Lone teleworking may be a solution for organisations with a problem of skill shortage, which normally leads to a network of employed teleworkers. Alternatively it may be a solution for individuals with a desire to experience the rigours of self-employment, offering their services to a range of clients.

- Teleoutposts are another option for the organisation with skill shortages or accommodation problems. Like lone teleworking, this form remains an adjunct to the conventional offices of the organisation, but differs from lone teleworking by grouping staff together. This may make management more accessible, and address any issue of isolation, but it may not have the same penetration into the skills pool of an area, as there is still a requirement for travel.

- The teleco-ops are the new wave of business forms which variously muster skills in rural or urban localities and market them nationally. They will provide solutions to conventional organisations by offering a managed, yet sub-contracted resource. Additionally they can provide a community of clients and a community of spirit by providing shared resources in neighbourhood locations.

- The tele-organisations have developed without the constraint of a conventional organisation, in terms of buildings. Their main assets are people, and the management skills which allow them to operate and coordinate staff and projects without the need for continual proximity to each other. This allows them the freedom of a very clear marketplace orientation.

Part III
Planning for Telework

INTRODUCTION: HOW TO PROPOSE, SET UP AND MANAGE A TELESCHEME

There is now a sufficiently wide community of experience in telework to support new initiatives. Teleworking is no longer a novel means of work organisation, and though it is still very much a 'minority sport' it is a realistic option for many organisations. The chapters in this section illustrate how to go about it.

7

Making a Teleproposal

Will the innovations you hope to accomplish be viewed as desirable by many key people in the organisation? If you're trying to convince top management that telecommuting will save space but corporate HQ is only 80 per cent full – you'll have a tough sell.

Professor Gerald Gordon

Successful implementation of teleschemes requires perseverance, determination, commitment, persuasion and power in the organisation. No one person is likely to have control over all these, and even the charismatic chief executive is almost certain to need to do a lot of persuading in order to penetrate a barrier of senior or middle management reserve.

The job of middle ranking managers in trying to sell the notion, especially those without line management responsibilities for their own section, is probably even harder. Especially where there is likely to be reserve or even hostility, a meticulous case needs to be prepared.

But this is not always so. In most of the schemes reviewed in this book a small number of key players have driven the projects ahead. Both FI and CPS grew from small beginnings, and the Windsor and Maidenhead project employs only five people.

The guiding principle seems to be to start small, consolidate, gain confidence and grow. There is nothing new in this principle; as Gill Gordon and Marcia Kelly commented in their guide to telecommuting: 'When companies started to use PCs their first orders weren't for 500 machines.'

In this chapter you will get to know how to evaluate and prepare a teleproposal. Several main issues need to be considered, and these are discussed below.

- Why telework?
- What culture?
- What option?
- What price?
- Which jobs?
- Which people?

- Which format?
- Why not me?

WHY TELEWORK? PROBLEMS AND OBJECTIVES

The notion of sitting at home in complete control of one's time, working at a leisurely pace, without the bind of commuting is an issue that has captivated the press. Link this with the fascination of the world of computing and telecoms, and the attraction of telework is overwhelming.

But taking along a press cutting to a management meeting is probably not the way ahead. Teleorganisation works by solving a clearly identifiable problem or exploiting a tangible opportunity. Clarifying the problem or opportunity is stage one. Stage one – cast your mind back to our track records.

- The Frontline Initiative sees an opportunity: to take work to inner city areas, and improving the IT skills complement.

- Enfield saw a problem: how to administer the community charge?

- Back in 1962 Steve Shirley turned a problem into an opportunity: by delivering work to those unable to conform to the 9-to-5 routine.

The checklist in Table 7.1 may help you to clarify the focus of attention for your scheme. Clearly a high proportion of 'Yes' responses indicates the need for some movement from the current *status quo*. Telework may be a solution.

In planning a teleproposal, isolate a specific problem which affects your management team. Use these questions to guide your search. Ignore the numbers in the first column.

Table 7.1 Why telework?

	QUESTION	ANSWER	
		Yes Quite significantly	No Not really significant
4	Do your staff complain about interruptions?		
1	Have you lost good staff due to short or long-term disability?		
4	Are there office jobs which could just as easily be done at home?		

2	Are there jobs where 'freedom from the office' would be beneficial?		
4	Is your office accommodation cramped or unpopular?		
1	Is early retirement popular?		
3	Do you have annual peaks and troughs in the work load?		
4	Does your staff complain about commuting?		
2	Are you faced with expansion but cautious about incurring further fixed investment in office space?		
4	Are you concerned that office productivity is not as high as you would like it?		
3	Do many of your employees live in the same area, with a reasonably long commuting time?		
2	Are your current office leases approaching termination or renewal?		
4	Do you believe you need to improve communications within your department?		
1	Do you have difficulty in recruiting and retaining the right skills?		
3	Does your department's work lend itself to part-time schedules?		
2	Is there pressure on office equipment usage?		
3	Do you have a high proportion of staff with families of school age?		
1	Is there a pool of retired people, possibly ex-employees, whose skills you would like to access?		
1	Do many of your staff leave to become carers or raise families?		
4	Are you constantly having to push staff in order to meet deadlines or output targets?		
3	Could you use the opportunity of an office move or re-furbishment to look again at work organisation?		
2	Could you earn more from letting all or some of your existing office space?		
2	Could you expand in another locality and exploit the cost gradient away from London?		
1	Can you anticipate skills shortages for certain jobs?		

Using the reference number in the column preceding the questions, analyse your 'Yes' reponses in each category.

Total 'Yes' responses

1	Staff recruitment & retention	
2	Office space/cost considerations	
3	Organisational or social change	
4	Motivation and productivity	

Copyright: Steven Burch Associates

The questions lead to four areas of focus:

■ Staff recruitment and retention

■ Cost of accommodation and overheads

■ Desire to facilitate organisational or social change

■ Concerns about motivation and productivity.

Equally, a hefty 'No' vote might reassure you that you do not have to contemplate fundamental change, and that either the problem as you see it is too diverse to be tackled in this way, or that there is a more appropriate solution.

WHAT CULTURE? THIS COULD BE RIGHT FOR YOUR ORGANISATION

Traditionally hierarchical bureaucratic organisations might not seem ideal targets for telerevolutions. This is a myth. For example, the number of local authorities becoming involved in telework is increasing. Besides Enfield and Windsor, Hampshire County Council has been piloting a scheme for over two years. The joint computer department of Sutton and Kingston Borough Councils is set to establish a substantial data processing teleoutpost in Barnstaple.

Being aware of the conventions and norms that apply in the organisation simply means that the proposal can be sold internally in the right fashion. A key consideration has to be the management style, and level of development of systems of measuring performance by deliverables. Where these are not so well developed, then you may have to significantly boost the training input to managers, but more about training later. The checklist in Table 7.2 is a review of issues you might consider in putting together and positioning the proposal.

Table 7.2 Management culture checklist – positioning your proposal

	Yes	No
Is your organisation capable of creativity and innovation?		
Was your last proposal for change well received?		
Are the decision makers clearly aware of the problem or opportunity you are trying to address?		
Do you need to sell the idea to individual managers before making a full presentation?		
Have you considered objections and been sympathetic to counter viewpoints?		
Have you found an ally in another organisation prepared to champion telework for you?		
Has there been a successful pilot project of any nature run recently in your organisation from which you can learn?		
Do the unions need to be sounded out?		
Is the organisation accustomed to using sub-contract work?		
If you anticipate a hostile reaction, is there one manager who might try a project?		

In the research for this book, 24 organisations wrote to explain why they thought telework in any of its forms was not for them. Typical reactions were:

> These schemes are not appropriate to our staff. Not suitable for this industry, nor I suggest to the oil industry as a whole. I find the concept fascinating; unfortunately the nature of our administration does not lend itself to remote working. In our view flexible working schemes such as teleworking are not productive enough for our management style.

These are likely to be positioning statements which may bear little rigorous analysis, and are probably throw-away comments from people who have either failed to grasp what telework is, or are so bogged down with their own organisational problems that they have no time to investigate the possibilities. You may need to temper your enthusiasm for your teleproposal in anticipation of similar reactions from those within your organisation. Their throw-away comments might mean that your proposal is also thrown away.

WHAT OPTION? 'WINDOW GAZING' AT ALTERNATIVE STRATEGIES

Telework may not be the answer. There will be some job functions, and types of business, for which it is difficult to find a telerole. For a Mayfair-based advertising agency, geographically close to is major clients, populated by creative people who thrive on chaos, telework could be the kiss of death, at least in some jobs. City-based firms of solicitors within walking distance of their clients may take a similar view, but individuals might in reality be able to organise themselves well enough to spend perhaps one day a week at home. Similarly, the size of the problem and number of people involved could be so large as to make a telework experiment too risky, or inconsequential in the light of more major changes, when for example 500 staff are being relocated.

If you have done your initial evaluation correctly then there may be a range of alternatives which stem from the particular mix of issues facing your organisation. Other options may be more appropriate. Job sharing may work for staff at all levels from clerical to managerial, where travel time is not a real burden. Creche facilities might be a solution, as might be the use of contract staff.

WHAT PRICE? THE HARD AND SOFT COSTS OF TELEWORK

Some evaluation of the cost and benefits will probably be necessary. If only as a benchmark, you need to know the costs of your current method of work provision. Can you measure the supposed benefits? Are you willing to reward those who join you in taking the initiative in their departments? As Gerald Gordon says, 'if you can't measure something – you can't count it; and if you can't count it, you can't tell how much it has improved.'

Evaluation of such a project could embrace the following considerations.

This is an imprecise art, and must at least attempt to address the costs and benefits of the options.

Cost the *status quo*

Ensure that you include your current recruitment and retention costs. Estimate, if you can, a cost for lower productivity as a result of absenteeism (the 'I'm not really that ill but it's a hell of a way to the office' syndrome) and working in a busy office.

The cost of occupancy was highlighted in Part I of the book and this may be a relevant consideration in your decision-making process, but almost certainly you will have to give consideration to other cost headings.

Equipment costs

Bearing in mind the relatively low level of IT equipment in use in most teleschemes where a phone, word processor or personal computer are the most common pieces of equipment, and also that the employer either has these or needs to provide them anyway, it is not easy to make useful generalisations about costs.

However, as computing and telecoms hardware prices continue to tumble, the range of availability will increase. But for employers, particularly of those in home-based teleschemes, utilisation of the equipment may never match that in a conventional office, where it may be available to multiple users.

Setting up a home-worker with a powerful PC, fax, laser printer and perhaps a photocopier, and completely refurbishing the back bedroom, could almost certainly be met on a budget of £12,000. Most of this cost would be incurred if the worker were to be office-based.

Transport costs

Taking the work to people rather than people to work sounds cheaper, and in most instances it probably is. But there are provisos. First, many teleworkers are required to visit their offices perhaps once or twice per week, and indeed their managers may be involved in more frequent home visits. Occasional office visits may play havoc with the economics of season rail tickets, meaning that no savings are possible here.

Second, as is true for Enfield Borough Council, there may be an immense amount of paperwork to be shunted around. Many schemes still rely heavily on postal or courier services.

Clearly before the complete trade-off can be guessed at, the cost of telecommunications needs to be taken into account.

Telecommunications costs

Since the British Telecommunications Act of 1981, the road to liberalisation in the telecoms industry has gathered pace. The first tranche of Cable and Wireless shares was offered later that year, and by February 1982 the group had established and obtained an operating license for Mercury Communications to compete with BT.

This competitive element was the beginning of the transformation in UK telecoms provision, which now means a greater choice in terms of equipment and services for UK users than in other Community countries.

In order to gain some perspective for the telecoms costs in typical telework situations, consider the rough estimates for two schemes.

The first is a long-distance remote unit, with a high level of data transfer to the head office, and a requirement for on-line access, and the second is a telescheme with home-workers in the local area, requiring voice contact and some data transfer.

In the first example, the British Telecom Kilostream annual charge for a 64 kilobyte circuit between London and Newcastle-upon-Tyne would be of the order of £7,000 per annum. This would provide dedicated and simultaneous on-line access to the mainframe for up to about six operators depending on the peripheral equipment at either end. They would also need office space at, say, £20 per square foot – say, 100 feet per member of staff. The office space/telecom equation for the remote office is therefore a total of £19,000 per annum. The office space alone in central London on a similar basis might cost £50 per square foot. The total of £30,000 makes the remote option about 37 per cent cheaper.

The second example envisages a home-worker operating within the local call area. Talking to the boss in the office would cost about £2.11 per hour. If on-line access was required for more than about two hours per day it would be sensible to consider a dedicated line, which would then give access 24 hours per day – particularly useful for downloading information. So, for less than £2,000 per year, the home teleworker could have a dedicated line back to the office, open all hours, all year. The actual solution for the telecoms link will probably lie somewhere between the two, ie about £500 for the hour-per-day public network link, or £2,000 per year for the dedicated circuit.

We may not yet be able to compete with Hong Kong or parts of the United States in benefiting from free local calls, but it is true for many organisations that the cost of telecoms is not a major factor in any decision to reject teleworking.

Management costs

Telework can transform the role of the manager, but more of this later. Quality rather than quantity of management ought to be the prime indicator, and where the focus is turned on the output of telework schemes, rather than on close personal supervision, one might expect the manager-to-staff ratio to fall.

In practice there are reasons why this might not be the case. First, when telework is new there is likely to be a flurry of mangerial involvement. Second, as managers adapt to their new roles they may find themselves travelling more in order to keep in contact and maintain their coordinating role. This may mean more management.

Perhaps the FI group provides the best example of higher management-to-staff ratio. In that company it is about double that in most other UK data processing companies.

Management expenses are likely to be higher, as their role will inevitably involve a greater degree of time and expense away from the company premises. Staff meetings will be held in hotels. Lone teleworkers will be taken out to lunch, perhaps to counter isolation. Managers returning to the office after a client meeting may take the opportunity to drop into the remote office or teleoutpost, and thus require an overnight stay.

Relocation costs

Specialists in relocation, PHH Homequity, found in their recent annual survey that more than 70 per cent of the 200 employers they questioned were spending between £5,000 and £15,000 per employee on relocation. The CBI puts the average figure at about £10,000.

The need to recruit new staff, company reorganisation, internal promotion and relocation of the entire workforce are cited as the major reasons for the moves.

Employers are having to re-think their relocation packages as the cost of moving people around soars. There is an increasing resistance to move as house prices stagnate or fall and other pressures come from unexpected quarters. British Aerospace in Plymouth experienced considerable resistance from employees in Bracknell who were encouraged to move as part of the company reorganisation. One of the most often quoted reasons was the desire to avoid any disruption to their children's education, once locked into the new GCSE examinations system.

One way of re-thinking is to consider teleorganising on a temporary or permanent basis, as a solution for even only a small proportion of staff.

Pay

Establishing a telework scheme based on paying less than the going rate has been described as yet another way of 'shooting oneself in the foot'. Most commentators agree. The main reason is image. Inextricably linked in the minds of many who might otherwise consider teleworking is that home-work somehow means low pay.

Perhaps because of this, most of the employee-based schemes do seem to offer common terms and conditions of employment to their staff whether home- or office-based.

However, especially where the contractual arrangement is on a self-employed basis, the evidence collated in the Empirica telework survey indicates that, in general, senior staff unencumbered by child care commitments or disabilities are most likely to benefit from the telework arrangements, while low-level clerical staff, especially women with young children, are likely to be less well off than their office-based colleagues. One of the main reasons for this is not so much that the 'rate for the job' is less, but that continuity of work is not guaranteed.

Productivity

Effective teleworkers are more productive than their office-based contemporaries. Few commentators would disagree with this. Just how much more depends on which of the anecdotal accounts one cares to read, but claims of anywhere between 20 and 100 per cent are made.

More is said later about productivity, but for now the implications on the headcount budget are at issue, and though it is realistic to expect a greater return from teleworkers there is not much hard evidence to quantify this. Nonetheless it is easy to see why the tele-environment has potential for greater efficiency.

First, there are fewer time thieves – the workmates, bosses, pesky customers, and one's own staff who show a blatant disregard for both their own and your time management. The typical office environment can be a pretty hostile place, as indicated in Figure 7.1 opposite.

Second, the tele-environment, at least when it is home-based and where the nature of the work allows it, can accommodate workers' own biorhythms, allowing them some freedom to work when they feel they are at their best. Underpinning this freedom is the prospect of very short commuting time to the work space, in stark contrast to those long, boring or stressful journeys to work.

But one should not be too influenced by these claims without further investigation, for work output in certain clerical and administrative functions is often measured in only a rudimentary fashion, making compari-

Kall Kwik Printing (UK) commissioned Sue Keane, a consumer psychologist, to design a survey – 'Office Irritations' – and conduct it at the 'London Secretary Show' in April 1989. 312 secretaries drawn from 17,000 visitors were interviewed.

89 per cent complained about being constantly interrupted when they are busy, which indicates a high level of stress in many offices. Other Top Ten Office Irritations cited by the secretaries included bosses being too demanding, having to work with smokers, photocopiers constantly breaking down and being considered the office dogsbody.

Least irritating factors included everything from poor office cleaning and small desks, to sexual harrassment. Sexual harrassment came bottom of the office irritations and, although 75 per cent denied that it was a problem at work, a worrying 25 per cent were irritated by sexual harrassment.

Most of the Top Ten Office Irritations were environmental or related to selfish colleagues but 69 per cent of secretaries complained that their photocopiers were unreliable, inadequate or old, while 72 per cent were irritated by the amount of time spent waiting for repairs. Standing over a photocopier annoyed 68 per cent of secretaries. Add this to the 68 per cent who complained about a new office irritation – the fax being constantly engaged – and it is easy to see that technology can be more of a hindrance than a help.

TOP TEN OFFICE IRRITATIONS RESULTS

1. Being constantly interrupted/distracted by others
2. Boss too demanding
3. Too much noise in the office
4. Photocopiers breaking down, being too old or inefficient
5. Office too hot, too cold, too stuffy or draughty
6. Having to work alongside smokers
7. Lack of communications with the boss and colleagues
8. Office too small or overcrowded
9. Being everybody's dogsbody
10. Not being given enough respect/responsibility

Source: Kall Kwik Printing (UK)

Figure 7.1 The hostile office environment

sons very subjective. The other danger to avoid is the tendency for the proactive and often productive aspects of office work to be siphoned off into the telenetwork, leaving the phone interruptions and other chaos in the office, making any sort of comparison futile and unfair.

Nevertheless, it would be an exceptional operator of a telescheme who was unable to report a satisfactory increase in productivity.

Cost or opportunity?

In part, at least, individual or organisational attitudes to telework are likely to be influenced by the level of economic activity. In periods of stagnation or modest recession the interest in telework is likely to stem from a search for cost savings. The intervening years of the 1980s have been boom years, and the focus has shifted from cost control to looking at the opportunities telework can offer to organisations in search of staff. It could be, therefore, that telework could always play a significant role in the organisation of work, irrespective of the prevailing economic climate. The reality is constant, but the motivations and numbers of those involved may well change.

Cost the future of doing nothing

You need to ask the question: 'What will happen to costs if we simply react to the symptoms? ' Bolstering the current arrangements may prove to be even more costly in the long run with, for instance, the need to pay extra salary weightings, free or subsidised parking and meals, higher recruitment and retention costs, and higher training and induction costs if you have to lower the entry qualifications in order to attract new starters.

This second stage may be highly speculative and involve considerable crystal ball gazing, but there are usually signs in the economy which indicate trends if not absolutes. For example, office rents in central London are predicted to soften somewhat at least in the short term, which may ease the pressure to a degree.

Having said this, if the situation is of concern now, the prognosis for the future is probably bleak, and even if office rents are easing, the difficulty may be in filling them.

Formulate and cost your teleschemes

Working space will be one of the biggest issues. Lloyds Bank have exploited the cost gradient out of London and substantially reduced their costs from £60 and more in London. Indeed, one of the criteria for locating their teleoutposts is that the prevailing rents in their target areas must be less than £10 per square foot.

The home option, some would argue, is a sneaky way of selling a cost as a benefit. With a rental of approximately nothing, the home office could be a great attraction to employers! Interestingly, telehomework in particular breaks many of the conventions about whose purse carries the cost of being at work. For example, transportation costs (of getting the work to the worker) are shunted to the employer, but the employees are effectively providing their own office accommodation.

Offsetting the cost of lower space rental will be higher communication costs, and not simply telecoms costs but the costs of remote meetings, the potential for additional accommodation and travel costs associated with managing the telenetwork.

Increased productivity is a reasonable expectation from most schemes, but this may be a long-run gain after a period of settling in, and big investment in manager training.

Attempt to forecast your future staff recruitment and retention profile, if you continue to operate in the same fashion. Costs in both these areas should fall in teleschemes, provided that they are managed well and create loyalty.

Finally in the wide ranging cost-benefit analysis, remember that successful teleworking brings considerable kudos and considerable publicity to the organisation. Lloyds Bank estimated that by January 1990 the Newton Aycliffe operation had gained them about £100,000-worth of free publicity.

WHICH JOBS? A CRITICAL LOOK AT WORK DIVISION

Stand back, try to look objectively at what goes on in the office, talk to people about the components of their job, ask them if they need to be at their office desks in order to complete all their tasks, and you may well begin to see that work and offices happily coalesce into an environment with a heavy social influence. Because of this you may conclude that for some jobs, or at least some portions of jobs, the office is positively the worst place in which to be.

In your trawl throughout the organisation you may find that you need to cast the net very wide indeed if you want to explore all the potential for teleorganising. It may be much easier in some ways to start by ruling out options. And always remember the guidelines will alter depending on the type of scheme you have in mind.

For example, to all intents and purposes a teleoutpost may be simply a branch office carrying out a range of tasks complementary to those in the main office. But setting up a teleoutpost in this way is an opportunity for change, and allows you to hive off into the back office those jobs suited to the particular environment, such as word processing, data processing, design work or clerical work, which require minimal access to those outside the organisation. The various Lloyds programmes are developments of this particular theme.

Most of the literature points to jobs in a range of functions as being suitable for telework:

- word processing and software documentation
- programming and systems analysis
- data entry
- consultancy
- clerical work
- management.

You will notice straight away that this generic list covers a vast range of jobs. Treat it merely as a shopping list – it takes you to the right aisle, but you have not decided precisely which brand to choose. Kelly and Gordon point to three criteria which will help to narrow down the search:

1. Tasks that are easily measured. They have countable or observable outputs and clear deliverables. For example data entry, employment interviews, financial analysts, training course design. They go on to stress that:

   > Jobs with hard to measure outputs aren't always bad prospects for telecommuting however. If a boss and sub can agree what is a good day's work, OK. As a job becomes less measurable, management discomfort increases.

2. Tasks that require little unscheduled face to face contact. Get people to analyse their use of time in the office. Weaning people away from the 'firing line atmosphere' can be a problem.
3. Tasks that don't require frequent access to files, equipment or suppliers.

Typically there are six characteristics for successful remote work:

1. Minimum physical requirements. Home space particularly is at a premium; many telejobs require electronic access to centrally-held files and data sources. Those that require more elaborate storage or space requirements are probably unsuitable.

2. Individual controls of own pace of work. One of the key attractions for many lone teleworkers is the freedom from the 9-to-5 routine, allowing considerable scope for choice in when to work. Many project-based tasks with longish time horizons are ideal for this. This does not preclude jobs with daily targets, but they may need to be sensitively designed in order to avoid excessive monotony.

3. Defined deliverables. Most managers will want to see jobs which have defined outputs, for example where data entry clerks are paid by transaction or where programmers work on a fixed price contract. This may work well, but may be part of the managers' concern over the loss of the privilege of direct supervision. There are successful time-based schemes such as CPS, but there are of course built-in long-term measures of performance and performance appraisal.

4. Need for concentration. The required amount of concentration is inversely proportional to the level of segmentation in the job. For example, routine data entry may have so many repetitive task prompts (numbers of batch sheets, insurance claims etc) that little concentration is required. Working on a project or report may require a great deal of concentration.

5. Defined milestones. Uncharted time needs managing. Long-term projects may need to be delivered to the teleworker with inbuilt progress milestones, in order to maintain high productivity.

6. Low need for communication. The productivity gains in telework stem largely from the isolation of the worker for periods of time. Hence, where jobs require limited communication, or where those interchanges can coincide with, for example, the teleworkers' office day, the greatest benefits are likely to be available. This does not rule out telework in jobs which have a high need for frequent and often reactive contact with others; it just means that these elements of the job are probably not best carried out remotely.

The checklist in Table 7.3 overleaf may help you to consider suitable jobs for teleworking as you trawl the various departments. The first stage is to rate each of seven dimensions in the job on a scale from low need to high need. One criterion for the relative gradings might be the amount of time involved for each of the criteria. Once the ratings have been estimated, they can be transferred to the Telejob Profile summary in Figure 7.2. You may find this a useful way of holding the details.

The summary is a start rather than a finish to the survey. You may have to go back to question staff more thoroughly on certain of the dimensions. However, you may well find several jobs which lend themselves to ready teleorganising: for example, those jobs which are immediately and

Table 7.3 Which jobs? How to begin a trawl of the organisation for telejobs

Attempt to rate each job according to the following seven dimensions, based on a scale from 0% = Low need to 100% = High need	
	% Needs rating
1 **Equipment** The need to have constant access to a large number of expensive or bulky items	
2 **Materials** The need to have constant access to a large mass of paperwork or other raw materials	
3 **Storage space** The need for a large personal storage requirement, say more than one filing cabinet	
4 **Uninterrupted time** The need to remain undisturbed by colleagues or customers etc in order to be efficient	
5 **Group work** The need to be in regular, unscheduled and immediate contact with colleagues etc	
6 **Reactive mode** The need to be constantly available to deal with ad hoc queries and directions, on a face to face basis	
7 **Defined deliverables** The degree to which the job can be satisfactorily measured in order to gauge productivity	

Copyright: Steven Burch Associates

completely transportable. These are the jobs which can be carried out almost entirely on a remote basis, probably from home.

Similarly, your analysis may take you beyond merely transporting jobs into a remote environment. It could be that the staff working in your

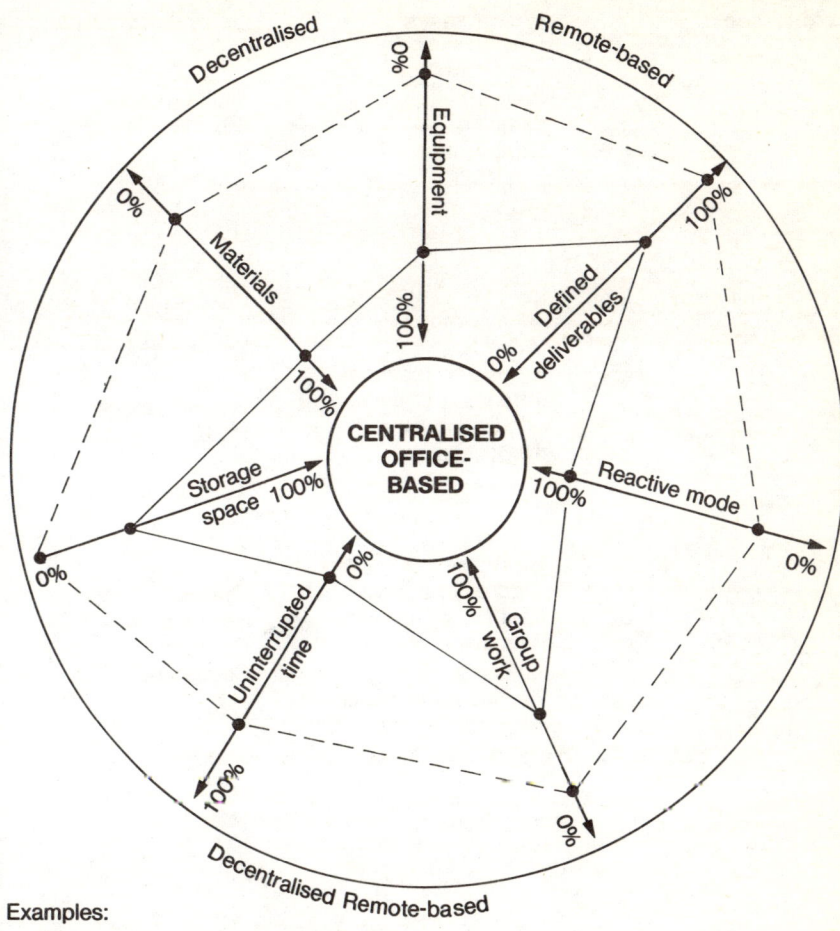

Examples:

Hatched profile = training consultant
Solid profile = receptionist/secretary

Figure 7.2 Telejob profiles

offices are engaged in a range of tasks, some of which are not best suited to the environment. The jobs may have evolved in this way as a result of technological or organisational constraints which no longer apply. In other words, they might be anachronisms. In order to carry out this second stage of analysis, it is important to estimate how time is spent by staff in each of three work modes.

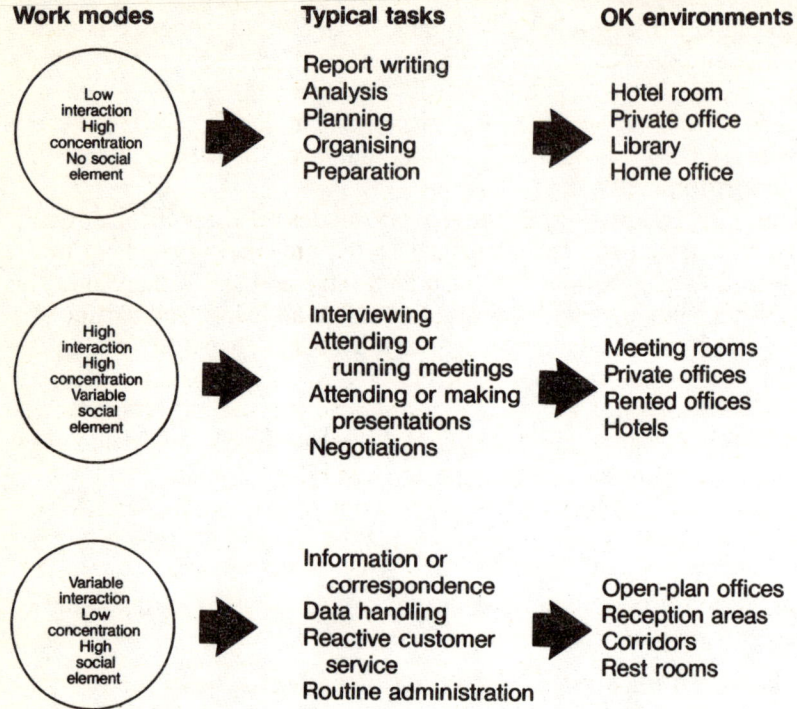

Figure 7.3 Work modes, tasks, and environments

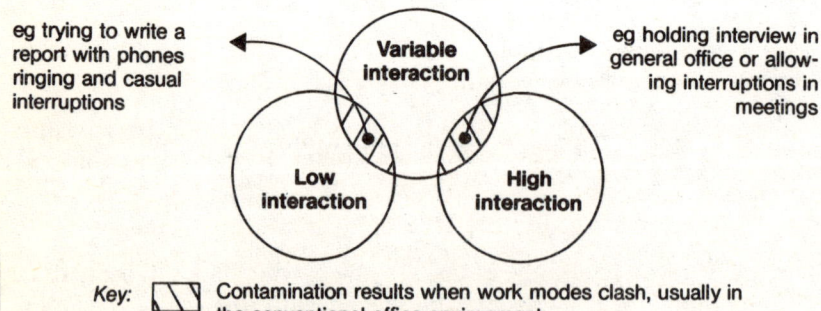

Figure 7.4 Contamination of work modes and environments

These are the jobs in which the job-holder has a great deal of interaction within the organisation but which have proactive components requiring planning, and periods of undisturbed concentration. There is possibly a further work mode which involves the need for more casual and unplanned collaboration with colleagues. The mix of these elements will vary from job to job, and can best be achieved by mixing office and remote environments.

Figure 7.3 opposite links these work modes to their ideal environments. Notice that the tasks themselves require varying levels of interaction and concentration, and may also have a social dimension. The boom in time management training for staff at all levels, and particularly those with proactive elements in their jobs, helps people to develop the self-discipline to control their time. Many of the problems occur because the nature of their tasks is often at odds with their working environment. Think of this as a contamination which undermines efficiency, and often leads to frustration and dissatisfaction (see Figure 7.4 opposite).

It is important to measure the components of the working week which could be categorised into these work modes, as this becomes the basis for evolving job design away from the office. Other than for the straight transfer of jobs from the office to the remote environment, there are two further possibilities (see Figure 7.5 overleaf):

■ Which jobs have a definable telework element? The route here may be to leave the job largely untouched, and offer the job-holder the prospect of mixing the working week between the conventional office and any of the teleschemes discussed earlier.

■ Which jobs could be re-designed to segment the two work modes completely? This is an opportunity to allow individuals to focus on particular aspects of the job, and possibly to shunt some of the back-office activities to an area of labour supply. Lloyds Bank have done this successfully on a national basis, and Enfield Borough Council have managed this successfully at a local level.

Before moving on to consider who ought to be the telepeople, use this survey to take advantage of any other opportunities in the business environment. Remember, one of the key attractions for employers is the perceived ability to better handle fluctuations in the workload. Calendar cycles often lead to lose/lose situations; staff up for the peaks and you have organisational slack in the troughs; ignore the opportunities to staff up and you miss valuable basis.

Teleorganising is one means of trying to work towards a core and community sort of structure, which incorporates a range of employment and

TELEWORKING

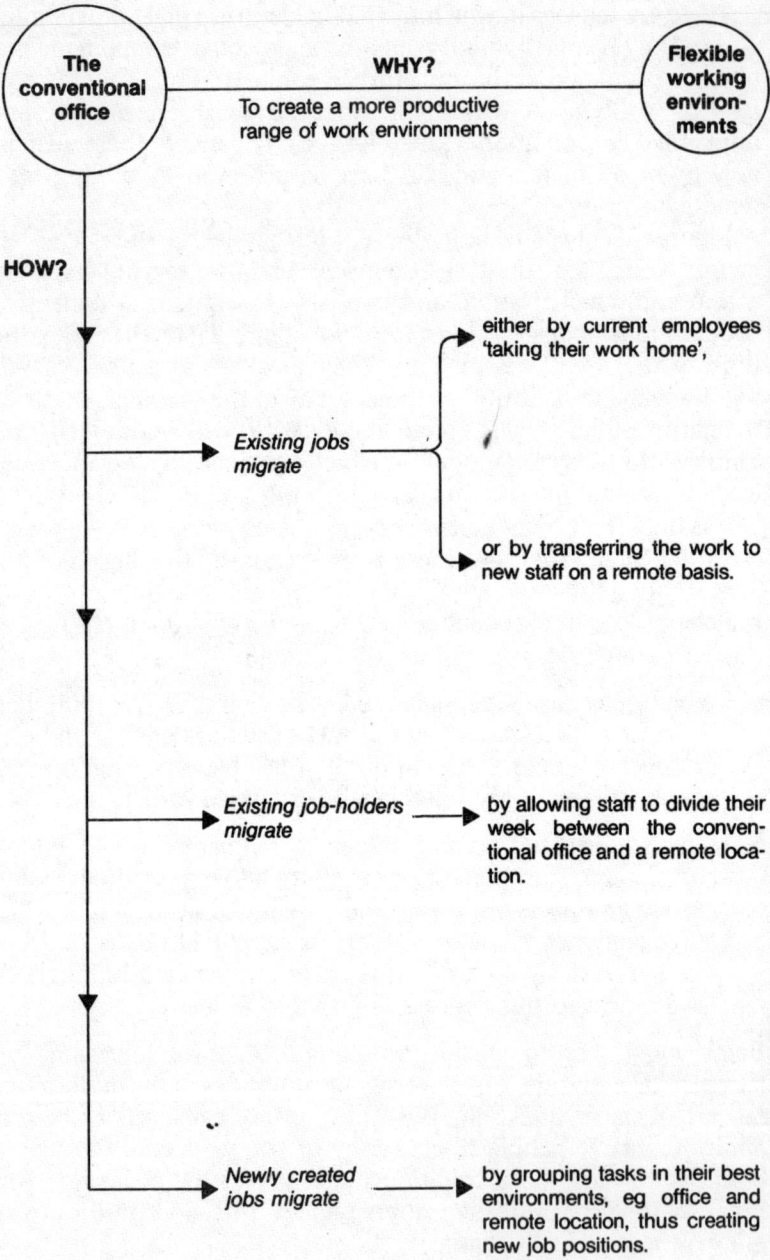

Figure 7.5 Routes to greater productivity

self-employment methods of providing work to individuals in order to benefit them and their supporting organisations.

There may be tremendous scope for a telerevolution in your organisation, but remember – in the early stages stick to easily definable problems and solutions.

WHICH PEOPLE? MOTIVATIONS, ASPIRATIONS AND TEMPERAMENT

Teleworking, especially when much of it is done at home, has some unique aspects. Other forms of telework, such as in teleoutposts, have fewer specific demands on those working in them.

Let us concentrate on the high home component telejobs. Kelly and Gordon point to what they call 'the unique demands of home working':

■ working alone for long stretches at a time;

■ working without easy access to co-workers, managers and other resources;

■ working in a physically comfortable and familiar setting;

■ working without the formal and informal cues for planning and time management that exist in the office;

■ working with more latitude about hours of work;

■ working amid friendly yet serious sources of interruption and distractions – family members, neighbours, TVs, stereos, delivery people.

Coping with these issues is something at which the seasoned teleworker becomes adept. Nonetheless, as part of the selection procedure it is probably possible to identify traits which will help those who are successful to cope with the new form of work. Potential teleworkers can only anticipate how they will react. As a manager you have to be satisfied that you think they might be right.

Francis Kinsman in *The Telecommuters* attempted to define the characteristics of a good home-worker, based on responses from people actually working in this way. The list of factors is presented here, in descending order of importance, but take note that the first criterion – that of self-discipline – was the clear favourite.

■ Self-discipline: the ability to sit down and get stuck in, even though other circumstances make it difficult.

■ Effective time management: the ability to plan, to set standards and to stick to them.

- Dedication: home-workers must be keen volunteers committed to success for financial or ideological reasons, liking the work and liking the lifestyle that goes with it.

- Ability to work alone: a liking for initiative, self-dependence and self-reliance which enables the person to survive having little personal contact other than on the telephone.

- Confidence, both in one's own abilities and in being able to ask for help.

- Ability to communicate.

- Technical experience.

- Flexibility and adaptability.

- Trustworthiness.

- Professionalism with clients.

- People skills.

- A quick mind.

So, you might think, what's so special about the home environment? Aren't all these things just as necessary in the office?

Many of them are, but perhaps the key requirements from which the others flow, is the self-discipline, and self-reliance which are necessary when all the normal office rituals and prompts are absent.

During the selection procedure, 'behavioural interviewing' may give valuable insights into a candidate's suitability. This technique explores the behaviour of candidates in past situations as a means of predicting how they might react in future.

So in looking for evidence of self-discipline, the interviews might explore instances of where applicants have successfully completed projects on time, or where they have worked without continual supervision. Evidence of this sort need not necessarily come from the working environment, and it must always be remembered that a vast majority of telerecruits, depending on the type of scheme you have in mind, may be women returners, whose organisational ability will no doubt have been most recently developed in the home environment.

Once you have considered the make-up of the potential teleworker, you need to consider where to recruit them from. There are several key considerations.

- Should they be from within or outside the organisation? There is no hard and fast rule, but there are different consequences. People brought into a telescheme as their first contact with the organisation will need a much more thorough induction and ongoing communication with the centre, in order to maintain their involvement. Conversely, employees who are allowed to take their work home may know their organisation well, but will have to cope with the new environment and the adjustments they will have to make there.

■ They have to be volunteers, but the decision about selection must be yours, not theirs. You are unlikely to have a dearth of applicants for a well though-out scheme. Telework recruitment, like any other recruitment, ought to be the responsibility of the line manager. You cannot afford to allow poor selection to jeopardise your pilot.

■ They have to be good, but not all that good. If you hive off all your best workers into the teleproject, the results will be biased and you may leave the office a little exposed. Remember that both management and other employees will probably have a vested interest in the project and you therefore need to ensure as far as possible that a scheme which involves selecting from a pool of existing office 'inhabitants' fulfils two criteria:
   — where the telework project is testing the new form of organisation, *as an alternative* to office-based work, that the scheme allows a basis of productivity comparison between the office and the remote environment;
   — that setting up the scheme does not adversely affect the running of the office; in effect the office environment becomes the 'control' for the telescheme.

■ Selecting from current employees might have the benefit of ensuring that the new teleworkers know the organisation and the people involved. Conversely you may be exporting some of the procedures and attitudes you would rather not have taint your new network. Teleorganising can be a way to introduce new practices and procedures.

A final note about telepeople. Nothing has been said about sex or age profiles. Chapter 1 dealt with the workplace in flux and suggested that work may be delivered in radical ways in order to meet the needs of men and women. Traditional roles (men go to work, women raise families at home) have probably never been as idealised as the model suggests. Indeed, there are more women at home caring for aged parents today than there are caring for children under five.

Telework can work for men as well as for women. However all common sense, and the reality to date, dictates that for the moment the vast majority of applicants are likely to be women. More on this topic in the next chapter.

WHICH FORMAT? FROM TELEOUTPOST TO LONE TELEWORKER

The likely options for diversification into telework from a conventional organisation, are to set up either a teleoutpost or a network of lone teleworkers. There are several initial questions you need to ask, which are intended to allow you to correctly position your proposal before working out the detail. For example:

■ Is your organisation ready to face the prospect of having people based at home? Would a teleoutpost which has similarities with a conventional office set-up be more acceptable, especially if you are already running a branch office network?

■ Is your pilot too small to justify setting up a teleoutpost, and would a number of lone teleworkers be sufficient to provide the information you need?

■ Could you make use of existing facilities, perhaps, by renting or short-leasing space in an established business centre?

Remember, that in order to sell the proposal, it has to offer a solution to a clearly identifiable business problem. The second part of selling the proposal must be to decide on the correct format for the telework pilot. For example, the need to hold on to the skills of several key individuals may only be addressed by working towards a home-based solution. Conversely, if the need is to process a high volume of repetitive data input, the teleoutpost probably provides the solution in that it allows the project to tap into low cost areas, and yet retains an office-based environment.

WHY NOT ME? A PERSONAL APPEAL FOR TELEWORK

You may want to propose yourself for telework, either as a precursor for a larger-scale pilot, or more simply because you think that it will work for you in your job. There are several key headings to consider.

Job content

You need to keep a personal time log of just how you spend your working day. How many of the tasks you undertake could be completed away from the office? How much of your job is reactive, possibly requiring easy and frequent access to colleagues? Is it possible to reorganise your week to group together the proactive elements of your job into a transportable day or two at home? You need hard data, collected over several weeks, before you approach the boss.

'Hook' the boss's interest

Find a valid reason why the boss should consider your proposal. Is office space at a premium? Could you suggest that two of you 'hot bed' a desk or an office for a trial period? Are you really a valued member of staff? Is the department being reorganised? Could your proposal give your boss some personal kudos if he or she were to take it on board?

Look at costs

Would your proposal mean duplicating accommodation or equipment? What are the telecoms implications? Consider what productivity gains there may be, as these may offset any up-front additional costs.

Help your manager

Do all you can to make the proposal easier to accept. Suggest this as a fixed term trial. Agree the basis of supervision. How much time will be spent in the office? How much teleworking? Ease the transition by suggesting that you work at an office bureau or leased office rather than at home.

Having worked through these stages you should be in a position to either make a plausible case for telework, or ditch the idea in favour of other solutions for your organisation or yourself.

8

Getting Your Scheme Off the Ground

Concentrate on only one or two key benefits to your firm. By choosing objectives linked to a problem that everyone can understand, you'll increase the chance of success because you're more likely to be surrounded by supporters not sceptics.

Marcia Kelly and Gill Gordon

In moving the proposal along to a working project you are probably going to need a lot of help and support, and you should think about a range of questions and issues which need to be addressed at this stage. Who should be involved in the final planning? How should we publicise the project internally and externally? Do we know enough about the psychology of telework? How should we train our managers and staff? What pitfalls are there in sending people home from the office? How do we make the best use of productivity? What are the benchmarks against which we measure success?

THE PROJECT TEAM – MATRIX OR HIERARCHY STRUCTURE?

Your organisation may well have a well structured approach to project management, regardless of the discipline. Because a telework project is not merely a technical exercise, in that it involves people, systems and organisation (PSO), a multidisciplinary matrix approach is best suited.

There are probably several groups of people who you need to work with – employees within the organisation, potential recruits from your newly created catchment area, external advisers and staff representatives.

Outside sources of help may come from telecoms and computing consultants, legal advisers, local planning authorities, central government grant schemes, trade unions, professional associations and the shared experience of others running similar schemes.

Any project team you set up to steer the process needs to have the

119

right representation. The nature and size of the project will influence the complexion of the team. For example, a project involving a tiny proportion of staff, set up in such a way as to be remote and almost invisible to those within the organisation as a whole, probably does not need a series of monitoring steering committees.

Ask yourself the question: 'What is the minimum number of key people who need to be involved in this process, in order to achieve success?' This should allow you to identify, at an early stage, those likely to impact on the programme either favourably or otherwise.

Then go on to ask: 'Of this group, who would be most useful in the project team, and who do I need to keep informed of progress, on a personal basis?' This approach could make sure that you capitalise on the talents of those interested in success within the team, and yet create some involvement from a wider audience who can influence the scheme, even at arm's length. It can also act as a damage limitation exercise, by keeping the potentially disruptive at least tethered to the project.

Potential team members may come from human resources, data processing, telecoms management, line management and, for example, estates management, as well as trade union sources. Remember that the majority of schemes will be concerned with the management of change, and this primarily means influencing people.

For example, British Telecom has just begun a pilot project, first to research and then set up a pilot-scale scheme, involving 16 directory enquiry operators. The research will cover issues such as the effects of technology, employment and management systems. The communications union UCW is involved in the working party to look at the research in more detail.

DEVELOPING THE PROJECT

Key stages in planning a successful pilot project include involving the whole team in clarifying the final objective, and then setting points within the process which describe the state of the project at that time. These are often called 'milestones' and are a way of expressing progress in the project in terms which ease the understanding of people who lack the fine detailed knowledge of some of the activities necessary in order to reach those milestones. They serve as checkpoints set throughout a project which ensure it is on course and which direct it towards its final objective, by stating what must be achieved without implying how to achieve it. For example, milestones in the project might be:

■   when teleworkers are ready to start work;

■   when remote office equipment requirements have been determined.

Note that these milestones are neutral with respect to the final objective. For example, if they had been stated as:

■   when the existing staff have been trained;

■   when typical home office requirements have been determined,

the implication would be that an employee-based home-working solution would be the outcome of the project. In other words such prejudicial milestones are not neutral to the outcome.

Reaching these milestones implies a great deal of activity, by individuals in the working party or by small sub-groups on specific tasks. For example, reaching the state 'when teleworkers are ready to start work', mentioned above, will require tasks such as selection, training, job definition and the setting up of procedures to be carried out.

Involving the whole team in establishing just what are the relevant milestones is crucial. Given commitment and agreement at this stage, the project leader's role as coordinator and communicator will be that much easier. Figure 8.1 overleaf gives an example of a typical milestone plan which should lead to some of the right decisions about a pilot-scale project.

MANAGING CONSTRAINTS

Attitudes to the provision of work, the legal and contractual issues which surround it, and the worker representation within it have evolved with the grouping together of people for activities in return for reward, in a master and servant relationship.

Here is another paradigm, and telework in certain of its forms seeks to challenge it. The key to the issue is the notion of employment, and the potential for problems arises when a particular teleroute seeks to cajole workers from this hallowed status.

There is a whole range of issues which manifest themselves when the boundary between employment and self-employment is reached:

■   How will the unions react?

■   What are the planning implications of home-work?

■   Will the Inland Revenue and the DSS notice the change?

■   What should the contractual arrangement be with our workers?

■   Who owns the equipment and is it insured?

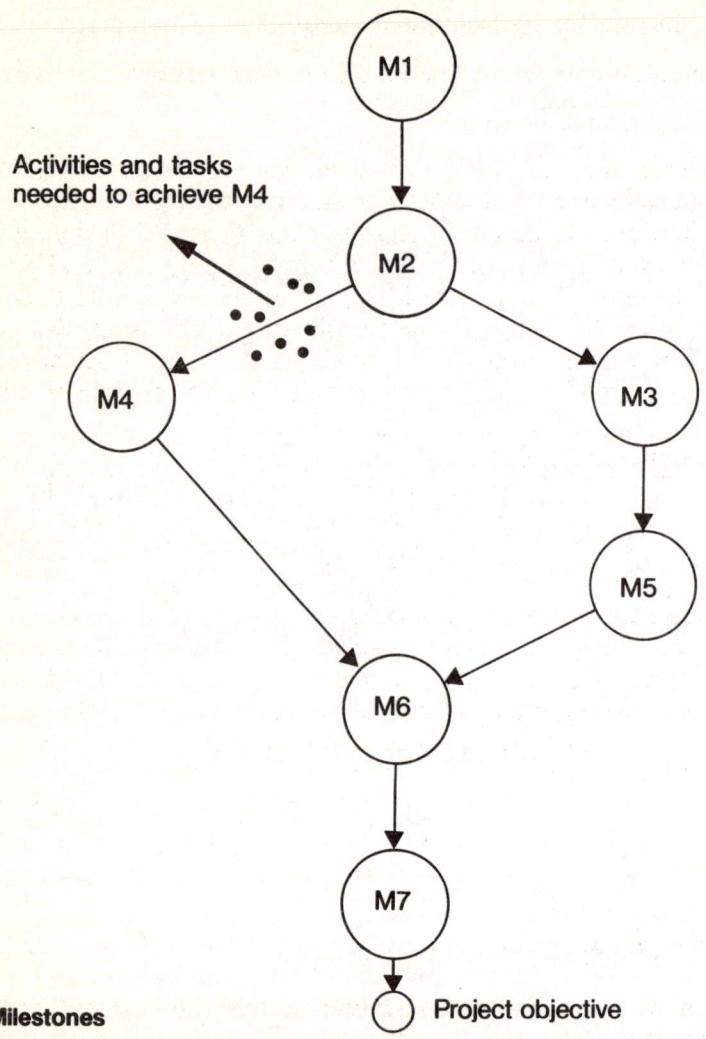

Activities and tasks
needed to achieve M4

Milestones

M1: When the project team is ready to start work.
M2: When the format of the telescheme which meets key criteria is agreed.
M3: When the telecoms and computing, and other equipment requirements have been agreed with the sub-group.
M4: When managerial staff are ready to take on the responsibilities of the telescheme.
M5: When telestaff are ready to start work.
M6: When criteria for success have been agreed.
M7: When results have been evaluated against the project objective.

Figure 8.1. Milestone planning for teleschemes

■ Who is responsible for health and safety?

■ How should we cope with the legacy of cheap labour?

■ Could teleworking be banned?

Before exploring these in a little more detail, however, we need to reflect on why organisations should want to break out of the employment convention. There are two groups of reasons. First, increased flexibility in coping with peaks of work, and reducing central facility costs and overheads may be difficult to achieve if employees are simply told to take their work home, yet remain in the payroll with all the perks. Second, employers may wish to attract better quality staff, some of whom may have a greater desire for self-determination which they believe self-employment would bring.

Organisations have a choice and there are many factors which ought to influence the decision but, as benchmarks, consider CPS and the FI Group – both successful, both in the same broad business area, both teleorganisations. The difference is that in the main CPS has followed the employment route, and FI the self-employment option.

In practice many people running teleworking schemes have had minor skirmishes with the law, planning authorities, or collective representation as their schemes have unfolded, but rarely have these been so great as to halt their progress. With a degree of careful planning and forethought, consultation and flexibility, the obstacles can be worked around; the key is to ensure management commitment internally to the process.

For many of the schemes discussed, self-employment is not an option in some forms of telework; in those where it is, however, let us look at the main issues.

Contractual status and the Inland Revenue

Once you have decided on status, make sure that the law, the Inland Revenue and the DSS agree. Any statement that teleworkers are self-employed is likely to attract their interest. The law remains imprecise as new forms of work organisation continually irritate its boundaries, but fundamental to a decision on employment status are, for example:

■ the degree of continuity of supply of work;

■ the number of providers of work;

■ the provision of equipment.

Figure 8. 2 overleaf is extracted from the Inland Revenue current guidelines on the determination of employment status.

If you can answer 'Yes' to the following questions, it will usually mean that you are *self-employed*:	If you can answer 'Yes' to the following questions, you are probably *an employee*:
■ Do you have the final say in how the business is run?	■ Do you *yourself* have to do the work rather than hire someone else to do it for you?
■ Do you risk your own money in the business?	■ Can someone tell you at any time what to do or when and how to do it?
■ Are you responsible for meeting the losses as well as taking profits?	■ Are you paid by the hour, week, or month? Can you get overtime pay? Though even if you are paid by commission or on a piecework basis you may still be an employee.
■ Do you provide the major items of equipment you need to do your job, not just the small tools which many employees provide for themselves?	
■ Are you free to hire other people on terms of your own choice, to do the work that you have taken on? Do you pay them out of your own pocket?	■ Do you work set hours, or a given number of hours a week or month?
■ Do you have to correct unsatisfactory work in your own time and at your own expense?	■ Do you work at the premises of the person you are working for, or at a place or places they decide?

Figure 8.2 Employed or self-employed – guidance from the Inland Revenue

Source: HMSO © 1989 IR56/N139

CPS, at one period, had to clarify the contractual position of its staff; in their view they were self-employed working on a sub-contract basis but, in the eyes of the law, CPS were their sole providers of work and thus in reality their employers.

Conversely, FI has to guard against becoming involved with the tax affairs of their panel members as this would draw them closer to an employed status. They use loans for the purchase of equipment as a means of consolidating the self-employed status of members.

Insurance

Broadly speaking, responsibility lies with the employer, so self-employed teleworkers will need to review all their arrangements for insurance. This may include contents, professional indemnity, permanent health, pensions etc. Work at home may, technically speaking, invalidate the normal comprehensive householder's policy, but informing the insurers of the change of use of part of the house may be sufficient.

Employed lone teleworkers need to be assured that their employer's policy cover extends to their homes, and does not in any way prejudice their normal house and contents insurance.

Health and safety

Much the same is true in the area of health and safety. Again telework has caught out the law. Employers have, of course, a statutory duty to ensure a safe workplace for their employees, 'as far as is reasonably practicable'. There is debate about whether or not compulsory intrusion into a teleworker's home is reasonable. All common sense says that it must be, in that there are other valid reasons why the employer should need access to the teleworker's home.

Enfield Borough Council intends to make a routine safety inspection of its home-workers' premises, and Digital Equipment Company Ltd in the UK has a policy document 'designed to provide health and safety protection for employees who conduct office-type work in their homes'.

The European Community has produced a Council Directive (90/270/EEC) which lays down minimum safety and health requirements for work with 'display screen equipment', and member states are required to introduce laws, regulations and administrative provisions necessary to comply with this Directive by 31 December 1992.

It requires employers to analyse workstations in order to evaluate the possible risk to the operators' health in respect of their eyesight, physical problems and mental stress. The Directive specifies the minimum conditions that any workstation should offer the person operating within it, expects the employer to plan the worker's activities in such a way that work on the display screen is periodically interrupted by breaks or changes of activity, and specifies the types and configuration of equipment which can be used, down to the details of the office chair.

Before embarking on a remote working programme design, any time devoted to the implications of this directive would be well spent.

Planning and other constraints

Central government in the form of the Department of the Environment and the Department of Employment are, generally speaking, sympathetic to the notion of the use of the home as a place of work. However, permission in this area still rests with the local authority.

Their attitude is likely to be formed on the basis of transparency of telework. The maxim, 'what the eye cannot see the heart doesn't grieve over' is usually their pragmatic view, so if telework fails to attract complaints from neighbours, the local authority is likely to take no action. Indeed many of them will encourage it, as a means of tackling their own resource shortages or because they support the concept of providing work into the community to those who might otherwise be deprived of it.

Taxation

The sting in the tail may well be the community charge. From 1 April 1990 self-employed people who work from home have been barred from making tax deductions on the basis of their community charge bills. Before then, property rates had been considered as a legitimate business expense which could be offset against tax.

Those working from home who took advantage of the law as it was, were also liable to pay capital gains on that portion of the sale of their homes which was entitling them to rate relief against tax. Presumably those who were claiming some rate relief realised they could be liable for capital gains, and had satisfied themselves of the relative benefits.

This may not have been a major consideration, but at any rate the change in the law means any option has been removed: no community charge relief, no capital gains liability.

The above comments relate to the individual community charge. Again, particularly for the self-employed community of home teleworkers, the issue of the uniform business rate has raised some concern. Are they or are they not liable?

The Department of the Environment Practice Note No 4 issued in May 1990 gives guidance:

> Property is domestic if it is used *wholly* for the purposes of living accommodation. But 'wholly' does not mean 'exclusively': and it is therefore considered that some non-domestic use is permitted without rates becoming payable if that use does *not* prevent any of the accommodation from being used for domestic purposes at any time. For example the use of a home telephone for a mini-cab service or as a call out number for a plumber would not attract liability for business rates. Similarly, a person might occasionally work at home, without preventing the property from being used entirely as living accommodation at the same time – by that person or someone else.

The Practice Note goes on to give examples of activities which might attract attention from the local valuation officer – a doctor's or dentist's surgery in one room of the house, a spare room converted into an office with office furniture and equipment, or a garage used to store tools and equipment. Such dual use premises are termed 'composite hereditaments', and the guidance note goes on to point out that:

> Despite a trend towards the increased use of domestic property for business purposes, however, the majority of composite hereditaments in the new rating lists will still comprise purpose-built business premises which also contain living accommodation.

The authorities involved in the administration of the business rate are the Inland Revenue which is responsible for valuation, the Department of the Environment which sets the rate, and the relevant local authority which has latitude within the legislative framework to decide on individual cases.

The legislation is new and subject to interpretation but, in any event, even if a home-worker were to be considered for valuation, this would be based on the commercial value of the portion of the house in question.

Obviously it might be prudent to seek the attitude of the local authority, but in reality it is likely to have issues other than those relating to home-workers on its list of priorities.

Worker representation

Opponents of telework fear the dispersion of the workforce, exploitation and loss of worker participation. They feel that decentralisation may lead to an erosion of collective bargaining rights. One of the realities of home-working in particular is that it tends to make union organisation rather more difficult.

It is reasonable to assume that employee representatives will react less than enthusiastically to any plan which will reduce the benefits to their members, or indeed diminish their power of representation. However, many teleworkers are also union members and it seems that there need not be any inherent conflict of interest.

However, to the TUC telework simply means an extension of more traditional home-work. Write to them and you will be forwarded their guide, *Homeworking – a TUC Statement*, published in March 1985. In it, the section on New Technology draws parallels with low-tech home-work, over which the TUC has justifiable concern: 'It does not mean that this new dimension has in any way supplemented or is likely to supplement existing areas of home-working as a concern for trade unions.'

Attitudes have moved on to a degree, and by 1988 Norman Willis, TUC General Secretary, speaking at the British Telecom/CBI Conference, was beginning to become more accommodating, acknowledging that unions had to: 'convince the teleworkers that they need us . . . [and] . . . devise new strategies for recruiting and representing teleworkers, such as telephone networks and newsletters'.

Huws and her co-authors found in practice that the involvement of trade unions in the introduction of telework 'has been negligible.'

The following are some of the constraints and attitudes to telework listed by the TUC in 1985 and opposite, some comments from 1988:

- Low wages – even computer staff who are receiving what are 'reasonable' wages for homeworkers are only getting about one-third of the hourly rates of freelance workers employed in the office;

- Extra costs at home such as lighting and heating;

- Loss of promotion and training prospects;

- Loss of side-benefits such as subsidised meals or social activities;

- Possible health risks, to all the family, from VDUs, machinery/chemicals;

- The effect on the family structure – for example, the stress on the family of the mother having to reach a deadline for the work at the same time that family problems need solving and individuals in the family seek attention;

- Loss of contact at work with other workers;

- The absence of trade union organisation to protect and further their interests in terms of pay;

- For those who are persuaded to become self-employed instead of employees, the loss of employment rights and protections.

THE TECHNOLOGY ISSUE

Always remember that teleworking is first about people and second about technology. In developing the scheme, the technology may be something of a side issue in that the appropriate decisions can be made by a number of key individuals in consultation with the group as a whole. The technological decisions, provided they are right, will always be more transparent than some of the organisational and managerial considerations, about which almost everyone will have an opinion.

Unless you are well versed in telecoms technology or you employ a

The 1988 TUC approach – *Health and Safety at Work*

Teleworking challenge to trade unions

The introduction of teleworking is a major challenge to the trade unions, who will find it much harder to recruit individuals at home than in groups and factories. In addition the unions' position as intermediaries between employees and management may be usurped by the line manager who could become the only channel of communication between the individual and the company.

TUC General Secretary Norman Willis, speaking at the September BT/CBI conference, acknowledged that the trade unions had to convince the teleworkers that they need us and must devise new strategies for recruiting and representing teleworkers such as telephone networks and newsletters.

Health and safety for teleworkers

Employed teleworkers are covered by the general (Section 2) provisions of the Health and Safety at Work Act. Self-employed teleworkers are only covered by Section 3, which states that employers have a general duty not to expose non-employees to risks to their health and safety.

Proposed regulations covering home-workers have been under discussion since 1980 but would be mainly concerned with the handling of hazardous substances by home-workers; clerical workers would be excluded. Ergonomic and VDU matters are currently subjects for guidance only from the Health and Safety Executive although a draft British Standard is under discussion.

telecoms manager, some of the developments over the last few years, which are growing at an exponential rate, may mean that the non-technically minded overlook some of the opportunities available. Refer back to Part I for an overview, and introduction to the technological issues, but consult professional advice in your decision taking.

THE PRODUCTIVITY ISSUE

Many administrative or professional-level jobs are made up of a range of individual and group tasks. In structuring your teleworking scheme you may be separating out the individually orientated tasks and exporting these to the tele-environment, leaving the group-based tasks back at the office.

One result is that much of the telebased work becomes proactive, concerned with achieving, planning and longer-range goal-orientated activities. In the office the converse is true. The work there becomes reactive, concerned with fire fighting, responding to customers both internal and external to the company.

Another result clearly is that the productivity in the different environments cannot be compared. In this scenario, the teleworkers will probably be streets ahead in terms of quantifiable output. In many schemes, the relevant question for teleorganising is not 'Are my telebased people more productive than my conventionally-based ones?' but rather, 'As a result of teleorganising, and taking into account the whole range of tasks, is my department more productive as a whole, and better able to cope with the diverse demands placed upon it?'

This approach is a positive one also in reducing any tendency for unhealthy criticism between office and telebased staff. Refer back to the Enfield Borough Council experience for their practical comments.

Productivity is closely related to morale and training, and it follows that these elements need to be properly covered if the scheme is to yield greater productivity. Nor is it realistic to expect an overnight transformation, and there may well be a slight fall-off in productivity as staff and managers cope with new systems, equipment and environments.

Why publicity?

You have a choice, either to communicate effectively the details of the scheme or to leave it to the grapevine. There is likely to be a great deal of interest in the scheme, especially if it involves any degree of change or disruption to existing work practices. Your policy needs to be clear and consistent. Staff may react with indifference or hostility if the scheme looks like being a threat to them in any way. One focus, where the scheme will involve teleworking for existing staff, may be to stress that:

- the scheme is an experiment for the staff and the company;

- no long-term decisions will be made before a full evaluation;

- the scheme may have advantages and disadvantages for staff and managers;

- it is not compulsory, but voluntary;

- full training is a natural part of the process.

Other schemes may not directly affect conventionally-based staff, and recruitment may be in completely different areas. However, if there is to be any working interaction between office and telebased staff then it will probably be necessary to keep staff involved in developments, even if only to allay any concerns they may have.

Finally, remember that too much publicity may draw well intentioned but harmful exposure. Your scheme will probably make a good news story for the local media, as it will appear to be new and radical (even when it is not). They will inevitably be looking for a headline: 'Local Firm Slashes Costs by Exploiting Home-working'.

This for example, is a factually accurate statement. Sadly it is confused by the implications of personal exploitation. It will make a good read, but probably not help your project much. As was true in the experience of Lloyds, local media interest can mean a great deal of free publicity, but it has to be managed carefully.

TELEWORK INSIGHTS

Young people at school often need some introduction to the world of work. They are unused to the rituals and environment. Those involved in preparing young adults for their first jobs arrange for them to spend time in the care of local employers; they arrange shadowing with senior people; they encourage links between education and industry.

You may have to do something similar with your potential teleworkers, as making the transition to the particular form of telescheme you are planning will require some adjustment, and probably to a working environment which they have never experienced and can therefore only imagine. Remember, most people know what an accounts supervisor or a sales representative does, but how about a teleworker?

The transition is likely to be most acute when the scheme involves home-based, lone teleworkers, but probably only when the transition is from the office. The Enfield scheme has demonstrated that incorporating work into the largely domestic life of lone teleworkers can broaden the lone teleworker's range of social contacts. A sensible programme for your scheme might include:

■ options to work at home, for perhaps one or two days per week on a purely experimental basis, but probably over a year or so in order to make the experiment more valid;

■ an open house forum where existing and potential teleworkers meet to discuss the particular issues of teleworking;

■ arranging visits to existing teleworkers in their homes, in order to watch the flow of work and begin to experience the home-work environment.

The key to designing telework insights is always to ask yourself the questions: Where are my potential recruits coming from? Do they need help in breaking the links with the office and coping with the new teleworking environment? Or is teleworking really bringing them closer to the organisation? In other words, see where they are coming from, and give them the support they need to cope with the new environment in which they will find themselves.

TELEWORKER PROFILES

There is a growing amount of statistical data available from which it is possible to make up an identikit of a typical teleworker. Table 8.1 shows the results of the Huws survey which analysed the sex, age and task of teleworkers, in various schemes throughout Europe. It gives valuable information on the way in which teleorganising is beginning to penetrate segments of the working population.

Table 8.1 Sex, age and task of teleworkers in Europe

	Data processing professional	Typist	Other professional	Other	Row Summary
Male (%)	32	–	65	3	27
Female (%)	77	7	12	5	73
Age:					
Up to 30 years (%)	72	6	17	6.	16
30–40 years (%)	68	4	25	3	60
40–50 years (%)	60	8	28	4	21
50+ years (%)	25	–	75	–	3
Column Total	66	5	26	3	100

(adapted from Huws, Korte and Robinson)

These results were based on a sample size of 116 teleworkers from 14 different companies across Europe. All the data are expressed in percentages.

These data seem to suggest that if you were to cram all the European teleworkers into a room and wander about in the dark, the odds are 3 to 1 that you would bump into a woman, 2 to 1 that the person would be a data processing professional, and 4 to 1 that you would have formed a new acquaintance with a person in their 30s or 40s.

As telework develops it will become more ubiquitous, encompassing a wider audience and range of jobs than at present. Each scheme is likely to have unique elements, and examples of a particular teleworker who breaks all the rules – such as the single, male, 25-year-old with no keyboard skills and a strong urge to be part of the group – will always provide exceptions to the rules.

But the information in Table 8.1 can be useful in targeting a group of potential workers for a scheme. For example, a scheme involving remote data processing is likely to find a ready market among females in their 30s, with caring responsibilties requiring much of their time to be spent at home.

DEVELOPING THE PEOPLE

Much of the focus will inevitably be on the people at the 'front line' of your telescheme, but what about that other important group – the managers?

'The three major obstacles to working at home are management resistance, management resistance, and management resistance'. This is the salutory warning of Paul and Sarah Edwards, Directors of the Association of Electronic Cottages in America, and it has a direct implication for the selection and training of managers for telework.

Your managers will break or make the scheme, and the special emphasis in telemanaging may expose failings in the managers themselves. A conventional workplace can harbour both good and bad managers, but a telescheme will soon sort out the wheat from the chaff.

One of the first principles seems to be that telemanagers must work in the same mode as their staff. Stuart Dennison at Enfield Borough Council has also recognised this need, and his 70 or so lone home-workers are supervised by a team who are themselves home-based.

Another principle is to ensure that the management reserve is broken down by appropriate training. Telework will catch out managers who are weak in basic key management areas, and training in these may become part of their individual development programmes:

- planning and scheduling
- effective communication
- delegation
- goal setting
- time management
- counselling and coaching skills
- performance review.

Courses in these topics do not necessarily have to be designed with telemanagers in mind, for they contain only the essentials of good management practice. Indeed, managers should be encouraged to work to their own solutions about managing at arm's length. There is little doubt, however, that the successful telework manager will have well developed interpersonal skills.

Fundamental to the new managing régime in teleschemes is the need to focus on suitable systems for judging performance by results, yet without getting too concerned about precise measurement. We have moved on from the age of scientific management. Telework forces a new approach, stressing the personal reliance between members of the network, with the manager acting as linking pin, in a new age of dependence management.

Training telepeople

From the chaos of the office, you may be offering your staff the tranquility of working at home. This ought to be good news, but for some it is an uneasy transition. Much of what follows relates to helping staff to make this transition successfully, but there are common elements which will help others in teleorganisations or teleco-ops.

For example, much of the training for a teleworker moving back home will relate to breaking some of the ties and conventions associated with the office. Conversely, the new recruit, working remotely from the main office, will want and need to know about the parent organisation, and to establish a network of contacts within it.

A comprehensive induction programme for lone teleworkers recruited externally is vital. Like every other employee, new workers need to understand the nature of the business, its values and methods of operating. Equally they need to develop the network of internal contacts in order for them to carry out their tasks. The manager needs to be clear about just who those contacts are, and then devise a way of ensuring they are consolidated.

In practice this probably means initial and ongoing contact with those people on site, and possibly linking the teleworker with a more experienced mentor who already has those contacts well established.

Unless you approach this induction from the teleworkers' perspective you may encounter problems. Remember they may be teleworking because they have limited access to the head office, or because of disability, caring commitments or transport problems. This may mean transporting your staff, limiting the course to half-day, or one-day training modules, for example.

Introducing new teleworkers to their own home environments could prove to be harder. Let us look at the main issues.

Office rituals

'Going' to work at all is the start of the office ritual, and is the beginning of a whole series of automatic cues and prompts that tend to infest the conventional working environment: the ritual greetings at reception, the first cup of coffee, the opening of the mail, the social exchange with colleagues, and the ritual moan about the accounts department, or the sales people, or the state of the food in the staff restaurant.

Our conditioning extends to the way we dress, the way we speak to others in the organisation, and the way we use the journey to and from work as a buffer between our working and non-working lives. The string of prompts and cues (the walk to the coffee machine, the visit to the next department, the unscheduled call to see the boss) are all activities which actively programme our days, sometimes with little involvement on our part.

Indeed, most time management courses are geared to encouraging individuals to wrestle back control of their time from colleagues within the organisation, and develop a personal sense of time and self-discipline.

For the teleworker much of this external control and direction disappears overnight, and the result can be decidedly uncomfortable. What replaces the string of office prompts is a void of open time, largely uninterrupted, perhaps totally flexible, and almost certainly alien. What makes it worse is that the time slot is surrounded by the familiar home environment, in which all sorts of domestic activities are usually carried out.

It was Henry Ford who said that 'Thinking is the hardest work there is, and that's why so few managers engage in it'. Many teletasks have a large thinking or proactive element, making the teleworking environment often intensive and quite hard work. This can be a big shock, and for some can be terminal for telework unless the staff have been properly prepared. You need to train your staff to cope.

- Time logs. Before letting telepeople loose at home get them to run a personal time log for several weeks. This is not necessarily for *your* use, but encourage your staff to use it as a benchmark for their own output at home. Tell them at first that they will find it difficult to adjust, and not to worry if in the short term their output drops.

- Ritual transfer. Get them to take a few familiar artefacts from the office to their home – a clock or a wall calendar or a table lamp etc. Until they feel comfortable about it, get them to work exactly the same hours as they would at the office, including the breaks, as regularly as clockwork.

- Working clothes. Again in an attempt to ritualise their day, suggest to people that they wear their normal working clothes; they may feel they are cheating if they wear jeans.

- Buffer time. Encourage them to think about buffering home from work: simulate the journey by walking or driving to collect the newspaper rather than having it delivered; take the children to school; make a ritual of spending ten minutes in the garden before 'clocking on' – anything to help change into the work mode.

- Daily schedules. Insist on daily 'to do' lists, which help to break up the day into different types of activity, or which encourage staff to develop milestones in the day: for example the daily call to the office at 2.00pm.

- Develop communications. Make sure that your staff are contacted at least once a day in order to maintain the contact, even if this is merely a social call. It should not be allowed to look like over-monitoring. Ensure that staff get all the relevant newsletters, staff circulars etc in order to maintain the link with the organisation. Give someone the project of developing a telestaff newsletter which can become a chatline for staff. Encourage staff in similar geographical locations to set up support groups.

- Concentration lapses. Staring vacantly at the VDU is not particularly productive, but it does happen. Encourage staff to take a five-minute break if they feel their concentration wandering. Reintroduce prompts by giving them a 30-minute timer to break up the day. Challenge them to set their own 30-minute work schedules. If they like drawing wall charts, get them to log their peak outputs and encourage them to share their successes with their colleagues.

- Seal the biscuit tin. Unease, pressure, a tough problem to crack, or boredom induce the desire in many people at the office to have another cup of coffee. The walk to the machine may even clear the mind a little. At home, however, it is worse: you have coffee *and* a biscuit or its culinary equivalent, and for many teleworkers this can become a real irritation. See Figure 8.3 opposite for some practical advice on how to deal with these 'home comforts'.

These guidelines are meant to help teleworkers to break away successfully from the office environment. Within a few weeks, or certainly months, most people will give themselves a little more leeway with their starting and finishing times, perhaps by starting a personal flexitime system. They may feel less uncomfortable in jeans, and generally more confident once they have realised their own routes to greater productivity.

Family members

Adjusting to telework may present personal challenges, but those around

Question: How do you know you have become a tele-addict and need to get back to the office?

Answer: When you are eating two packets of biscuits per day and your clothes no longer fit.

What you can do is:

1. **Set targets** – schedule realistic goals. Even at a reasonable work rate you are quicker than in the office.

2. **Bad habits** – pin up a list of your domestic addictions; face up to them and substitute them with positive addictions. Take an exercise break instead of a meal break.

3. **Rewards** – spoil yourself when you achieve. Take a long lunch hour in town, talk to a neighbour or watch a TV programme.

Figure 8.3 How to avoid over-indulgence

the teleworker also have some adjusting to do. Mum or Dad really is there, the kids can see that, but they've been told that he or she isn't, and 'why couldn't you just pop down to the garden shed while your silly printer is printing?' Lack of understanding causes friction, and though the range of office distractions has been removed a whole host of others can take their place: 'If you're at home, couldn't you put out the washing? It won't take a moment.' 'Look, if you're not working why can't you nip down to the shop? I really haven't got time.'

Many teleworkers find tedious in the extreme the assumption that 'being at home' means somehow 'not being at work'. The teleworker has to explain to others in the home the demands of the job, and ground rules must be laid down about how to proceed.

- Encourage staff to have a 'council meeting' with their families to agree on issues such as the open/closed door policy, normal working times, and the procedure for 'emergency interruptions'.

- Get them to trade off wants and needs with each other: 'I'll make the coffee at 11 o'clock if you'll listen to me for ten minutes.'

- Tell your staff to relax, and not to worry about all that extra productivity they have been told about. They probably opted for working at home in order to be able to spend more time with their families. They need to learn to be ruthless with time, but gracious with their loved ones.

Being taken seriously

The reactions of friends and neighbours may surprise your teleworkers. Some will be green with envy, believing the arrangement to be a perfect solution to all their own working problems. Others will think your people have taken leave of their senses. But they will all show an interest in the 'novel little arrangement'. The same sort of deals as those struck with the family are needed, and perhaps one or two other tactics.

- Answering machines. Get your staff to leave them on during the working day so that they can choose to take, or not to take, incoming calls.

- Working hours. Encourage telestaff to talk about their regular working hours to friends and neighbours, in order to create a sense of their unavailability. They may not actually work those hours, but talking about them should reduce the interruptions.

- Easy targets. Your staff may suddenly find themselves very approachable by people in need of favours, such as letting the delivery man in, holding on to the key, watching the house while friends are away. Train your staff to be ready for this, and to learn how to say 'No'.

- Status. Tell your staff to prepare a stock answer for all those social occasions when people not very well known to them ask, 'Tell me, what do you actually *do* for a living?' Their temptation may be to say something like, 'Well I work at home in the spare bedroom, on a sort of part-time basis.' This will probably not help your staff to feel good about themselves, and they may become the subject of commiseration, sympathy, and probably unspoken ridicule. The trick is to prime them to say what they *are*, rather than what they *do*. So if they are the personal assistant to the chairman, or if they are local government officers responsible for community charge administration, get them to say so. If subsequently they happen to mention that they actually work from home, their working arrangements may then become a subject of great interest and envy.

The early months of your scheme could be an interesting time. Considerable readjusting will have to be done by both managers and staff. A great deal of monitoring, training and sharing of experience will be needed, and a timely review after six months will be of benefit. But once this honeymoon period is over, the work must still go on. Chapter 9 is all about managing over the long haul.

9

Managing Teleworking Schemes

Managers must become service brokers and evaluators of productivity and quality, not perpetual sheep-herders. The best way to achieve this relationship with telecommuters is to set out specific goals and timetables for each work-at-home project.

William Atkinson, 1985

Strangely enough, and in spite of the welter of comment in the literature, it is beginning to look as if managing on a remote basis is not quite as difficult as it seems. If managing is about making the best of available resources then perhaps the remote manager simply has to re-shuffle the pack of management skills a little, and play one or two aces differently. In practice this will probably mean that managers will need to develop and use their interpersonal skills to greater effect.

For any leader, managing people is a challenging task which requires a range of skills and a flexible style to match the needs of individuals at their various stages of development. Of a range of useful tactics, close supervision is merely one but it has almost totally overwhelmed the debate about remote management.

The belief that effective management somehow equates with close supervision is also one of the major reasons for managers rejecting telework schemes.

If general good management practice works, why devise a new set of rules for teleschemes? There is no good reason at all, but every cause to look at the main issues which tend to dominate in telework schemes, and how managers must review their approach and style.

WORK MEASUREMENT

Almost all companies have sales forces that work on a location-independent basis. Over decades, systems have developed which are clearly understood by all concerned, for measuring performance against results produced. The fact that the sales manager rarely sees his or her staff does not seem to be much of a hindrance.

No one, even outside sales, would think to comment on this form of work organisation as being anything other than appropriate. It seems perfectly normal. You might be surprised if the production manager were to comment to the sales manager, on this style of operation: 'Isn't that interesting? Aren't you worried because you can't see them or manage them in person?'

From this perspective the issue seems straightforward. Sales management has developed sophisticated techniques based on *infrequent contact* between manager and managed. Office management has evolved through a different process, where *ready accessibility* has been the norm, and where it might just be possible to muddle along without more formal procedures.

To re-distribute some of the conventional location-based work on a remote basis simply requires the manager to jump through two hoops: first to set aside the idea that simply 'being there' has any value at all other than in offering the manager a very cosmetic comfort factor and second, to refine or devise effective methods of work measurement.

Steve Shirley of F International explains their approach in terms of the monitoring they carry out.

> All the time we monitor – not only the job and how well it was done: Was the customer satisfied? but also how the workers performed: Were they accurate? Were they on time? Did they come up with ideas? Do they show potential for promotion?

These questions can only be answered with a vision concentrated on results and outputs. Relatively few jobs handled on a telework basis are time-dependent or with a high reactive element which requires immediate response to customers. Most jobs tend to be project-based, fairly well governed by accepted targets, or those where performance is measurable against standards on perhaps an annual basis. This means that they can all be quite closely measured, so that the focus for management can be on quality standards, monitoring of output, and problem solving with the teleworkers when required, but leaving them to get on with the job when not required. The fact is that in many schemes continuous or process supervision is not possible, leaving the evaluation of work results as the main supervisory activity.

Interestingly, in the Huws et al survey they report that the length of time worked is not measured in any way by many of the teleworking organisations, as a means of rewarding telestaff. But there are always occasions when time sheets or work diaries are necessary for client charging purposes, or for evaluation against the planning stage for contracts. Teleworkers in general identify with and prefer these methods of management, especially when they have had some input into the standards which apply.

Dependent on the job type, there is a range of output measures which will be appropriate.

Short-term work targets

Particularly for clerical, data input or telesales jobs, daily achievement targets may be appropriate. The objective in setting them is to provide a yardstick against which to judge individual performance, to allow more accurate budgeting for an activity to take place, and indeed to act as an incentive to the teleworker who may be experiencing difficulties with self-motivation.

The home-working telesales staff at Cox have a daily expected customer call rate of 40, and the staff administering the community charge on a home-work basis for Enfield Borough Council are developing targets for an acceptable level of performance.

Because the targets are short-term, possibly weekly or daily, they allow the individual teleworker the opportunity for immediate feedback on performance. They also allow you, as the manager, to pick up warning signs quickly when the performance of a staff member falls below par.

Project-based targets

Many projects which are not purely technical or procedural involve change and influence; they affect people, systems and organisation. Projects of this sort almost always require a great deal of interaction between people, and this can be handled satisfactorily on a remote basis. Indeed the practical difficulties in convening meetings between project team members, managers and perhaps clients, tend to mean they are fewer in number and more productive in outcome. Mike Kirby emphasises the need to try to transfer ownership of the various projects to his teleoutpost team. Part of the process is to encourage the team to set its own goals and deadlines.

Your primary role as manager from this point on into the project is one of monitoring and support:

- checking progress against project milestones;
- interaction with other project members;
- providing appropriate resources.

Long-term standards of performance

Many organisations use this method of reaching an agreed contribution by the employee. Because it is based on long-term achievements, and is usually a measure of the proactive element of jobs, it is entirely useful in telework schemes.

Similar schemes involve management by objectives, a technique used by Federal Reserve in the United States, which allows a work-at-home option. Management by objectives claims Duane Kline is probably the bank's chief insurance against abuse of the work-at-home option: 'If anyone were to goof off at home, they'd be sweating later to catch up in order to meet their annual objectives.' The psychology is simple:

■ devise interesting and realistic standards of performance or objectives;

■ get agreement and involvement from your staff in the setting of those objectives;

■ appeal to their instinct to achieve, and sell the idea;

■ agree the deadlines and delivery terms;

■ then, as manager, back off until the review date.

If this process has been managed well the responsibility for results lies with the employee, which is exactly as it ought to be. All the manager has to do from there on is to monitor, provide assistance as necessary, and wait for the goods to be delivered.

The Industrial Society, a national training and consultancy body, uses the technique widely. Many of the advisers working for the organisation work regionally and probably only visit their offices once or maybe twice per month. They do not use the term, but in fact they are teleworkers. In the main their work consists of servicing the management and staff training needs of their clients and developing new business. Regular monthly reviews are held with their line managers at which performance against the agreed standards is monitored. Typical standards might include:

■ revenue generated;

■ number of days' training;

■ number of client visits;

■ organisation of special promotion or event.

These might be annual standards, but are monitored regularly. Provided that the adviser is meeting these standards, which incidentally relate to the job and not to the individual *in* the job, the boss can be relaxed. How the adviser spends his time is not the direct concern of the boss, provided that the standards are being met.

The technique can be developed a stage further by introducing individual targets. For example, high flyers may be performing well above the standard for the job. The challenge here is for the manager to set individual targets for them in order to maintain job interest and commitment. Similarly new people, or people new to teleworking, might reasonably be expected to perform below the standard of the job, until the manager's coaching helps them to reach that standard (see Figure 9.1).

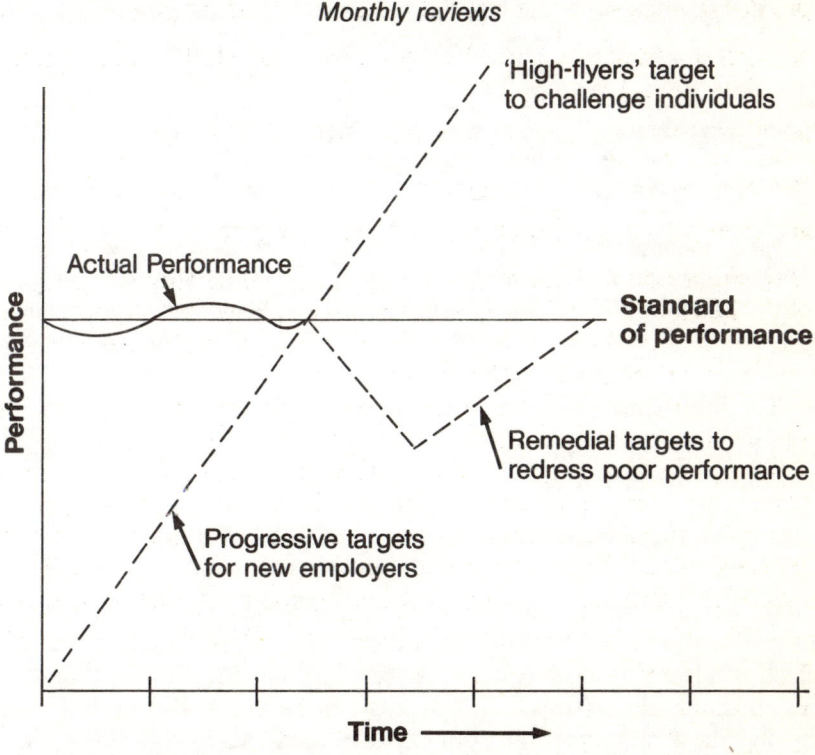

Regular meetings with staff managers can monitor performance against agreed standards, so teleworkers know how well they are performing and what is expected of them. Standards are constant for the job. Targets are set for individuals in order to allow them to achieve the job standard, or to provide a further challenge to high performers.

Figure 9.1 Managing by remote control

Job and key result area	Standard of performance	Individual targets
Telemanager maintenance and development of tele-network	To ensure no more than 5% of projects fail to meet quality criteria per year	To devise a new induction course for existing employees moving to telework, by 12 July
Programmer writing programmes	90% of programmes to be completed within original specification date	To design a new internal newsletter for other programmers in the network
Telesales person routine maintenance of client contact	To maintain an average of 40 calls per day	To increase sales of new product in area by 10% during the third quarter
Word processor written correspondence, reports etc	To average no more than 3 document corrections or revisions from head office per month	To design a new layout for the standard acknowledgement letter for customer complaints by 20 June

Note that standards and targets must be measurable, but can relate to numeric information, quality standards, procedures or deadlines.

Figure 9.2 Key result areas, standards and targets

There are few managers in the teleworking field who could relax without the confidence that the work measurement systems they operate were effective. Clearly, in developing a new scheme, modifications to standards in conventional working arrangements can be made. But do not make the mistake of simply farming out existing standards to your teleworkers. You will probably find that they can out-perform them by a considerable degree. Figure 9.2 illustrates standards and targets across a range of telejobs.

EMPLOYEE REVIEW

The previous section concentrated on effective and ongoing measures of work measurement. These may be important in the justification for developing schemes, and indeed may provide telestaff with the right motivations for their work. But it must remain true that work output alone is only one facet of employee review.

Teleworkers, like conventionally based staff, need due consideration of their own development needs, recognition of their personal aspirations, and to be kept involved in the working of the operation. Clearly the degree to which these considerations are important will vary between individuals. However, perhaps the best way to keep telestaff in tune with organisational goals, and for their managers to keep in tune with their staff, is to develop a formal appraisal or review system. Not only will this provide useful information and lead to agreements about past and future performance, but also it has the unwritten agenda of bolstering the impression in the minds of telestaff that they really do have a place in the organisation.

COMMUNICATIONS

'Is There Anybody Out There?' was a chapter title in Francis Kinsman's book which dealt with the progress of telework within several organisations in the UK in the mid-1980s. It can also be the plaintive cry of people *in* organisations surrounded by the clutter of everyday communications. Getting listened to, harnessing good ideas, checking out procedures and getting people involved require structures and processes, which are rare commodities in many organisations.

Nor are office buildings any help in this respect. Herding staff together in office environments is absolutely no guarantee of effective communication. Quite the opposite can occur, in that managers assume that mere proximity to their staff somehow facilitates effective communication. The reality is that staff are normally bombarded with information relating to the day-to-day discharge of their duties – the 'how' of work – but are very often kept in the dark about the 'why' of work, that is, information relating to the future, to changes, to new developments and to the way in which these might affect staff.

In the conventional office, the grapevine and the social hum of office life normally fills the vacuum created by management omission. But for the teleworker, especially when home-based, this neglect really does bring a new and damaging meaning to the term 'remote working'.

The way in which management is structured can have an impact. For FI, though they operate what they term as a 'conventional management structure' they are keen to emphasise a fundamental difference: 'We have replaced the office building with a structure of communications – electronically, by telephone, by post, in person – a structure that stresses our interdependence.'

Developing and maintaining the communications part of a remote working scheme is yet another opportunity to wipe the slate clean in management terms, and get at least the framework right at the outset.

For many people the working day is a conglomeration of activities requiring interaction with others, in the same office, the same building, or perhaps elsewhere in the case of clients and suppliers. Modern technology has increased exponentially the scope for each of us to transmit information. Sadly, technology is not so helpful in allowing us to assimilate that information in a user-friendly way. The net result is, usually, first a tremendous waste; second and more importantly in terms of productivity, the chaos that continual interruptions create.

Communicating task functions

What is perhaps surprising when we look at the range of communications methods used by those in teleshemes is the high proportion of non-IT methods used for the transfer of information.

Some schemes have a heavy reliance on telecoms transfer, such as the Lloyds Bank schemes, where leased lines and workers in teleoutposts provide the service to London-based staff.

The work of Huws et al shows that in the 14 schemes surveyed, over 80 per cent communicated by hand-written letter or other paper-based documents, and over 70 per cent continued to use the postal services.

Another scheme with a high IT bias is that run by Mike Kirby of Windsor and Maidenhead Borough Council, where again the work is transferred between the Civic Centre and the teleoutpost in Telford.

In contrast, Enfield Borough Council has a daily collection and delivery service as the main means of transfer between the Centre and its 70 or so remote workers in the locality.

Personal Computers or terminals are the commonest forms of hardware across all types of scheme, and while modems are used extensively for downloading information between computers, on-line use of modems for communications does not seem to be very widespread, at least in home-working schemes.

One conclusion is that teleworking is prospering without a necessary reliance on sophisticated IT for communications purposes. The new wave IT facilities, such as videotext and videoconferencing, are not in significant use. Even electronic mail is not a feature of many schemes, rating as an important element in less than 15 per cent of the schemes surveyed by Huws.

There appears to be a natural aggregation in the method of communication in the various scheme types. In the main the teleoutposts carrying out remote processing are linked by telecoms pipes providing cost-effective data transfer. Most of the schemes involving telehunters, lone teleworkers or teleorganisations tend to be less concerned with data transfer and therefore the requirement for open lines of data communication are not needed.

Here an evolution of methods meets the needs from postal services, telephone conversations, transfer of data by floppy disk, courier services, and personal collection and delivery of material.

Communicating 'maintenance' functions

Task detail is often about the 'how to do' of business life. Also, quite often it has a short-term time scale, related to deadlines, levels of output, routine dealings with clients' suppliers and other stakeholders in the business.

Superimposed on this communications infrastructure in the best run organisations is another level of dissemination of information, which usually has a longer-term perspective to it. Its focus is in helping employees to relate better to their organisation. It often attempts to open up the creative process, and begins to answer the question of why things are done the way they are. Communications of this type help individuals to maintain their involvement with their providers of work.

Without it, commitment, loyalty and the sense of purpose can drift. When teleworkers in the Huws survey were asked which aspects of their working environment it was most important to change, the need for improved communication with employer and colleagues was ranked higher than all other factors other than improved child care.

For many, particularly lone teleworkers, communications is seen as a problem. But for many managers it is a transparent one, with the hum and bustle of the organisation and their exposure to sources of information creating in their minds the belief that everyone else knows what is going on. It is a dangerous trap, common enough in conventional organisations but probably even more damaging in teleworking.

In referring to the track records in Part II we see that at Cox Pharmaceuticals the lone teleworkers are invited to all the regional quarterly sales meetings as well as to the annual company-wide 'get together'. And of course the regional managers and sales reps keep in regular contact.

Mike Kirby ensures that his staff at the teleoutpost in Telford are kept in touch by arranging regular liaison meetings, quite often at mid-way points, often putting aside a whole day to make this happen. He also spends time at Telford, 'probably slightly more than I might for purely business purposes'. Experience in running the scheme has shown him that communicating the purpose of the teleoutpost certainly cannot be done by memo or fax.

The local regional managers of FI are responsible for organising twice-yearly 'Freespeaks', where teams meet with their key managers. There is a common format to the meetings which are partly briefing, partly open forum and partly social.

Writing in *Industrial Participation* in 1987, Steve Shirley explained the process:

> The briefing is similar for each round. Overhead projector foils are used to illustrate the company's progress, and one or more managers may talk about plans of particular interest – career structures, training etc.

At the question-and-answer session, questions can be submitted in advance and anonymously but most come from the floor. In recent years they are assertively involved in the business and where it is going.

The social part of each freespeak includes little ceremonies like the presentation of gold watches or bracelets to people reaching ten years' service, minor announcements, and then some modest refreshments – typically wine and sandwiches.

For Lloyds, still in their honeymoon period, task-related communications have been developed to a fine art; the managers are routinely making every effort to keep staff informed and involved but are conscious of the need to make communications a high-profile management activity.

Support networks

Especially for lone teleworkers, the ability to pick up the phone or pop around for a chat with a colleague is important. Teleworking in all its forms tends to stress the interdependence of those engaged in it, and such self-help networks are common.

Most of the evidence, and common sense, points to the need for all teleschemes to include a systematic approach to communications. The best invest heavily, and the greater area of cost is not in the setting up of the telecoms infrastructure but in the amount of management time which has to be devoted to the process of developing and maintaining workable face to face communication.

EMPLOYMENT STATUS AND REWARD

Decision makers in organisations record two primary motivations in considering teleschemes. These have already been detailed; they are the ability to cope with work peaks, and the desire to attract and retain scarce staff.

A journey down these avenues has to include a debate within the organisation – 'To employ or not to employ?' seems to be the relevant question.

Taking out the peaks

Keeping the organisation 'light on its feet' in order that it can better cope with peaks and troughs of work is likely to lead it to consider contractual bases of work provision other than employment, with its associated fixed costs. This allows it to keep, develop and appropriately reward its conventionally employed core staff, and yet to allow it to retain flexibility and capacity within the marketplace by using sub-contractors, including teleworkers.

Pushing out work from the core to a flexible peripheral environment of non-employees helps the organisation to unburden itself from the overheads associated with sick pay, holiday pay, and pension and National Insurance contributions. The reality of course is that these costs, being significant, are going to be recovered by those contracting to the organisation by way of their fees.

Establishment costs (office space, heat, light, furniture provision etc) and others associated with redundancy, recruitment and relocation are also costs which an organisation may feel it can better control and even reduce by teleorganising.

When these are combined with the greater productivity reported in teleschemes, and with the prospect of teleworkers being able to offer the organisation greater knowledge or expertise gained from existence outside the conventional organisation, it is clear why some say that universal employment of its workers is likely to be both expensive and constraining.

Meeting needs – organisation and staff

Though the organisation may be clamouring to shed its fixed costs by developing a telenetwork, those people it wishes to attract may have none of it. If their skills are scarce, and they are therefore able to influence the negotiation, they may insist on employment. They may also insist on a flexible work option, but within an employed framework. This may include the option to work at home or, where this is not attractive or is impractical, to be allowed to use neighbourhood work centres, or business bureaux for at least part of the working week.

Others, including those in the organisation with a desire for what they regard as the headspace of self-employment, may consciously opt for this or may take the shepherding approach of the Rank Xerox Organisation. In 1982, with the prime aim of reducing overhead costs at the Central

London Office, they set up an experiment in which a number of executives were allowed to operate as teleworkers on a self-employed basis. The philosophy was that the networkers should run independent small businesses, but also perform a substantial amount of work for their parent company.

There are therefore a range of options to be considered in the decision-making process about the contractual status of telework. Whether the shift towards greater flexibility will mean the setting up of more schemes where full employment is not at the heart of the contract is a matter for speculation.

Where the skill requirement is in demand and is highly valued – probably at a 'professional' level, eg programming, managerial or creative work – individuals are likely to have the bargaining power to dictate their terms and conditions, which may mean self-employment. It may also lead in the direction of home-working, or perhaps teleoutposts.

Towards the other end of the skills supply spectrum, for instance in word processing or clerical work, the normal sort of telesolution will probably imply employment, possibly on a part-time basis, and will probably lead towards teleoutposts, where some of the social or community benefits of conventional office work can be re-created.

Given these likely trends, it seems probable that flexibility and cost savings in the 'professional' schemes will arise from some or all of the following:

- the use of staff on a self-employed, short-term or assignment basis;
- the reduction in overheads by replacing office capacity by home-work;
- the siting of teleoutposts in areas of lower labour or accommodation costs.

For clerical-based schemes, self-employment may be an unrealistic option but have scope remaining for flexibility and cost reductions via part-time or short-term employment, and the reduction in overheads by replacing office capacity by teleoutposts, and, as for 'professional' schemes, by the siting of teleoutposts in areas of lower labour or accommodation costs.

These considerations are guides rather than prescriptions for telework, and indeed the track records of Part II illustrate hybrid schemes including both employment and self-employment.

Pay

Inextricably linked with the status of employment is the issue of pay. Because of the historical perspectives that have tended to link the idea of home-working with female exploitation and low pay, any scheme which moves away from providing equivalent status to all employees is likely to attract criticism.

Catherine Hakim reported on the status of pay within home-working schemes in Britain, based on the 1981 survey, and concluded that while this was low, it was accounted for in large part by the short part-time hours typically worked. At the time she found that home-workers had hourly earnings concentrated disproportionately at both ends of the national earnings distribution. She went on to say that:

> two apparently contradictory conclusions can be drawn; home-workers are among the highest paid workers in Britain (one-fifth have hourly earnings in the top 10 per cent bracket), but they are also very low paid (over one-third have earnings in the lowest 10 per cent bracket).

It should be said that this survey included all types of home-working, including manufacturing which lies outside the newer wave of information-based telework. However, the attitudes which have been formed about home-work are flavoured by this reality, in particular the fact that in many cases home-work means cheap work.

Returning to the concentration of earnings distribution, it seems evident that supply and demand, as in the economy at large, determines control and reward in the teleconomy. Huws's later survey of European Teleschemes also concluded that earnings vary greatly. Other interesting conclusions made about telework and pay are:

- nearly 90 per cent of women work less than a 40-hour week on average. For the male teleworker just the opposite is true: nearly 90 per cent work at least 40 hours per week. These differences are clearly at least part of the explanation for the women teleworkers' low income.

- even when corrected to a full-time working week, there are three times as many women as men in the lower income bracket.

And, for data processing professionals,

- a disproportionate correction for part-time work would not alter the fact of reduced earnings in the group of teleworking data processing professional staff compared to the profession as a whole.

Equally important are the perceptions that teleworkers have about their level of pay. Quoting Huws again:

> The majority [of those surveyed] think that telework is financially disadvantageous. One in five believes that the loss in income is serious,

153

exceeding 20 per cent. One-third think that they are earning about the same as they would be on site. This leaves under 10 per cent of teleworkers who reckon that they are earning more than in traditional forms of work.

These findings can be quite depressing for those who are looking for telework to offer a symbiotic basis for meeting the needs of both the individual and the organisation. And, of course, these realities have been tremendously strong in forming opinions.

It seems that telework, when it is haphazardly introduced or poorly controlled, (or indeed is based on covert exploitation), can lead to lower rewards. It can lead to a polarization of the worst of employment practices present in conventional organisations.

From this perspective it is not difficult to see why, for example, the trade unions have found it difficult to shrug off a philosophical distrust of such schemes. But they, like the managers providing work for their members and potential members, are having to re-think the way in which work is delivered.

But if their pay really was worse as a result of telework, why should those teleworkers accept it? There are no doubt many reasons, but two important ones may be that:

■ teleworkers can offer employers a niche market. Seventy-five per cent of teleworkers are women, many of those with job options limited by family commitments. Conventional work, for many, is either undesirable or impractical.

■ less than one-third of teleworkers are the main earners in their household. For this group, high earnings may not be the top priority.

The practical point from this discussion is that any combination of reward, status or opportunity which creates in the minds of teleworkers an impression that they are less highly regarded than their colleagues in the organisation or their professional peers in the work community at large is almost bound to be counterproductive.

Robert Poulis, manager of a telescheme for a Dallas-based software house, commented:

> Remember all that extra productivity out there. You don't tap into that by creating second-class citizens. Savvy companies pay the same, treat the same, and even offer their telepeople the chance to come back to the office when they want to. That's how you get a return on your investment.

CONCLUSIONS FOR THE MANAGER

Managing a telescheme is different from running an office, and yet it is the same. By and large the people are the same, and the work to be completed may be more or less the same. What is different is the dynamic of interaction between those involved in the scheme and, for lone teleworkers at least, the loss of the ritual and comfort of the office environment. The degree to which a telemanager has to review his or her approach will depend on the scheme. Migrating work out of the office calls for different skills.

For example, as the manager of a home teleworking scheme you may find that there is much more travelling involved. Suddenly there is a requirement to get to know the members of your teleworkers' families, as you are likely to be bumping into them if you make home visits. Your time perspective may change; after taking the trouble to go to visit one of your teleworkers, you might go on to use the time more productively by making a working lunch of it – what was once dealt with in a cursory fashion in the office now becomes the basis for what, to all intents and purposes, becomes a business lunch; it may feel slightly alien at the outset.

If your telescheme involves the use of sub-contract working arrangements you will almost certainly become involved in financial or contractual negotiations. The briefing meetings you run may need to be managed better, and in spite of careful planning you may still feel, to some degree, a loss of control.

Running teleoutposts will mean more travel. You may need to become *au fait* with telecoms technology, and become much better at planning your time. Keeping staff informed of developments at the head office may become a routine and structured activity, and you may choose to build your team across several locations by meetings and perhaps 'exchange programmes'.

The loss of the office

As a telemanager you will have to sharpen your people skills. Having been banished from the office, lone teleworkers will be looking to you for support. The same may be true of those working from a distant teleoutpost where they may feel deprived of contact with the focus of activity. You may have talked it through with them and they will have tried to imagine what it will be like but, strangely enough, the first time your staff work from home they may be very uneasy, albeit in their own comfortable environment – the office discipline and ritual will be gone; the social contact will be missing.

Once you have helped them through these early stages, the initial discomfort and disorientation will be replaced, for those for whom telework is a solution, by the discovery of a great new working freedom.

The new dynamic

You are your teleworkers' lifeline back into their normal working environment, and they will be looking to you for support and encouragement. If they do not get it your scheme may fail, and it will be your fault. New recruits into a telescheme may suffer the same initial problems, and in some senses may suffer a greater anxiety as they will have little knowledge about the organisation at the end of their telecoms umbilical cord.

So, what are the implications for the telemanager? Those investing in success will be more trusting, more sensitive. They will be better communicators, will understand the importance of the monitoring and support of their staff, and will successfully coordinate the work of the telegroup. The result will be greater individual commitment, and increased group output.

The best managers have always put their people first. With less organisational clutter around them, putting people first is the best way to differentiate this new form of work organisation from its less productive stable-mates.

Part III: Key Point Summary

- In making a teleproposal, ensure that you have identified one or two key problems for which one of the forms of telework may provide a solution.

- When developing the proposal, avoid the obvious contradictions such as proposing to develop a local lone telenetwork when the conventional office is partly empty.

- Attempt to create a cost framework for your proposal, including the costs of doing nothing.

- In looking for the right jobs for telework, consider those with elements which require concentration and freedom from interruption. Also look at flexible work arrangements including telework and conventional office work.

- Ensure the right mix of interests and experience in your project team. Teleorganisation has a technological component, but managing people through the required changes will probably be a far greater issue.

- Ensure that appropriate training plans have been devised which will help both managers and other teleworkers to cope with the changes they will face. In particular, telemanagers will need well-developed interpersonal skills.

- Ensure that a fundamental of managing teleschemes is a sensitive system of work measurement and performance review. This not only benefits the organisation, possibly through greater productivity, but also the teleworker, who may find that it helps with issues of time control and the self-discipline required of, in particular, lone teleworking.

Epilogue

STRAIGHT FROM THE HORSE'S MOUTH . . .

This particular horse is the author's personal assistant. Her office is in Winchester and his in Devon – teleworking pure and simple.

I did not start teleworking for all the reasons given in this book, such as wanting to bring up a family – mine are grown and rapidly leaving the nest. I was looking for a new direction in my working life and this presented itself as a challenge, so here I am. My family have been supportive of my decision. I think my husband had visions of a sparklingly clean house and the evening meal on the table ready and waiting for him. He is a sadly disillusioned man!

Before leaving my previous employment, I found that some of my colleagues were quite envious of my new job, others (particularly the men) did their very best to dissuade me from teleworking. I took no notice of them, and happily took the plunge.

I am very fortunate that we have a spare bedroom for my office. Here I have my desk, filing cabinet, computer, laser printer, telephone and answering machine. It has been quite a challenge establishing my office and setting up the systems, but Steven (Burch) has been tremendously supportive.

The reactions of friends and neighbours have been interesting. Some were quite sympathetic, thinking I was doing this as a stand-in before finding another 'proper' job. Others seemed to think I would be hanging around the house with time on my hands. Working from home is, in the minds of many, synonymous with addressing envelopes or taking in washing, and only done by those who cannot do anything better.

One difficulty I hadn't envisaged when I first started working from home was separating *work* from *home* and on the days when I was not scheduled to work (I telework three days a week) I found I couldn't switch off from 'office mode'; I either did office work or wasted time around the house unable to settle into anything. I have overcome that by getting an outside job for my two extra days, and this extra job also fulfils my need to chat to people! I feel I now have the best of both worlds.

Working at home means no more rushing to catch buses and trains. There is time before work to give the dog a long walk, having waved off the aforesaid sadly disillusioned man on the 06.46 to London. There is also time for a swim before work on one morning a week. Keeping fit and keeping my hands out of the biscuit tin are important issues for me.

Working at home means I can dress in jeans and a sweater if I wish, although at first I used to dress up as if going out to work. Working on my own means I can have the window open without anyone complaining of draughts. Coffee breaks mean I can rush up the garden while the kettle is boiling to fetch in or put out washing, according to the weather. Lunch breaks can mean either watching *Neighbours* or tramping across the fields with the dog, depending on the weather and my mood. I have also found that working on my own means I have a better concentration span than when I was based in a conventional office.

I do still sometimes miss working in a conventional office. I miss the companionship – having someone around to use as a sounding board for work problems as they arise. As I now work for a rival company to my previous employers, I have had to start to build up a network of contacts (virtually from scratch). When I first started teleworking I felt lost, that I didn't belong anywhere, and that I had no job status. Now I have learned, thanks to Steven, to be really positive about the job, and I have convinced several friends that teleworking is the best thing since sliced bread.

We have found that good communication is the key to successful teleworking. The daily telephone conversation between base and teleworker, which keeps both parties up to date with what is going on, and enables us to discuss queries or problems, is essential. We also find it very helpful to meet once, or perhaps twice a month, in order to go through items of work which are difficult to sort out over the phone. On those days we make time to have lunch out together which gives us the chance for a natter, or to air, in a calm and relaxed atmosphere, any bones of contention we may have between us.

We have proved that teleworking can be a very successful way to run a business, be it between Lands End and John O'Groats, or even between Winchester and Devon.

Barbara Dunton
Winchester, January 1991

References and Further Reading

Several authors and books have been mentioned in the text. These books and articles have influenced me and are all worth reading if you want to take the subjects further.

Chapter One

The Henley Centre for Forecasting (1988) *The Development of Teleworking: An Economic and Cost Benefit Analysis*, report presented at the CBI/British Telecom conference 'Tomorrow's Workplace'.

Fayol, H translated by Storts, C (1949) *General and Industrial Management*, Pitman, London.

Report by the Institute of Manpower Studies (September 1988) *Create or Abdicate*, Witherby & Company, London.

Report by Institution of Civil Engineers (1989) *Congestion*, Thomas Telford, London.

Labour Market Quarterly Review (January 1989), Employment Department Skills and Enterprise Network, Sheffield.

Lloyd, B (September 1989) *Management Today*, Management Publications, Haymarket Press, London.

McGregor, D (1960) *The Human Side of Enterprise*, McGraw-Hill Book Company, New York.

Russell, P (1988) *The Awakening Earth – The Global Brain*, Arkana Books, London.

Spring Labour Force Survey (1988), Employment Department Skills and Enterprise Network, Sheffield.

Taylor, F W (1911) *Principles of Scientific Management*, Harper and Row Publishers, New York.

Weber, M (1947) *The Theory of Social & Economic Organisation*, The Free Press, New York.

Chapter Two

Forester, T (1988) *The Myth of the Electronic Cottage*, (Futures) Butterworth and Co, Sevenoaks.

Huws, U, Korte, W B & Robinson, S (1990) *Telework: Towards the Elusive Office*, John Wiley & Sons Ltd, Chichester.

Nilles, Carlson, Gray & Hanneman (1976) *The Telecommunications Transport Tradeoff*, John Wiley & Sons Ltd, New York.

Shirley, S (Summer 1987) *F International*, Industrial Participation, London.

Chapter Four

'Going Going Gone' (May 1990), Special Report on Relocation, *Personnel Today.*

Chapter Seven

Kelly, M M & Gordon, G E (1986) *Telecommuting: How to make it work for you and your Company*, Prentice-Hall International, Hemel Hempstead.

Kinsman, F (1987) *The Telecommuters*, John Wiley & Sons Ltd, Chichester.

Olson, M (1981) *Remote Office Work: Implications for Individuals and Organisations*, School of Business Administration, New York University.

Chapter Eight

Edwards, P & S (1985) *Working from Home: Everything you need to know about living and working under the same roof*, J P Tarcher, Los Angeles.

Huws, U, Korte, W B & Robinson, S (1990) *Telework: Towards the Elusive Office*, John Wiley & Sons Ltd, Chichester.

Chapter Nine

Hakim, C (1981) *Home-based work in Britain*, Department of Employment Research Paper No 60.

Judkins, P, West, D & Drew, J (1985) *Networking in Organisations*, Gower, Aldershot.

Kinsman, F (1987) *The Telecommuters*, John Wiley & Sons, Chichester.

Lawson, I (1989) *Target Setting*, The Industrial Society, London.

Shirley, S (Summer 1987) *F International*, Industrial Participation, London.

Index